FUN FARE

THE PUNCH BOOK
OF FOOD AND DRINK

FUN FARE

THE PUNCH BOOK OF FOOD AND DRINK

Edited by
Susan Jeffreys

Foreword by
George Melly

GRAFTON BOOKS
A Division of the Collins Publishing Group

LONDON GLASGOW
TORONTO SYDNEY AUCKLAND

Grafton Books
A Division of the Collins Publishing Group
8 Grafton Street, London W1X 3LA

Published by Grafton Books 1988

British Library Cataloguing in Publication Data

Fun fare: the Punch book of food and drink.
1. Humour in English, 1945–. Special
subjects. Food & drinks. Anthologies
I. Jeffreys, Susan II. Punch
827'.914'080355
ISBN 0–246–13404–6

Printed and bound in Great Britain by
Butler & Tanner Ltd, Frome and London

Red Bread by A. P. Herbert is reproduced by permission
of A. P. Watt Ltd on behalf of Lady Herbert

The following articles by Miles Kington: *Attention all Wine Drinkers*;
Bring on the Substitutes; *I'm the Chef of Araby* and *Mauvais Appetit!*
are respectively copyright © 1971, 1972, 1977, 1977

CONTENTS

FOREWORD
by George Melly

'Don't make jokes about food,' growls the eponymous hero of *Hobson's Choice* when his rebellious daughters tell him there is no 'proper pudding'. He would be just as indignant about the contents of this book, especially as it compounds the offence by making jokes about drink, an equal passion of Père Hobson. Salford would certainly have heard about it if he'd got his hands on a copy.

It isn't all jokes, however. It is, in parts, celebratory (marvellous meals), in others ruefully regretful (frightful hangovers). It scourges indifferent service, chemical adulteration, pretension, whether traditional or *nouvelle*, and hymns the pleasures of natural ingredients and careful preparation. It lifts a steady glass to the glow induced by moderate imbibing.

While the past is given some space – naturally enough the curate yet again extols the partial excellence of that famous egg – most of the material is quite rightly contemporary. Never have the British been so obsessed by food; as a topic of general conversation it has almost, hurricanes excepted, overtaken the weather. Yet this new-found passion for the pleasures of the table has, as you might expect in a race which remains at bottom profoundly puritanical, produced as much anxiety as satisfaction. At one time, with the exception of a few Francophiles, we just ate. My father was typical of his generation in resenting visiting a restaurant under any circumstances. It was considered extremely vulgar to praise or even notice what your hostess chose to put in front of you. 'Good value' meant lots, cheap. Wine, amongst the middle classes at any rate, was almost never considered, or else dismissed as a stuffy Victorian affectation. You ate, as a rule, what you'd eaten in the nursery – only at different times of the day. 'Good' and 'plain' were the two adjectives most often linked in advertisements for a cook.

Well, all that's gone by the board. The only pockets of resistance are old-fashioned clubs where Nanny still rules. No magazine or newspaper, with any pretensions beyond tits and arse, would dream of not employing a restaurant critic and a cookery writer. On top of all this we are bombarded with frequently contradictory advice on what is good and bad for us, harassed by dietitians, courted by health farms. No wonder tension has set in; and anxiety, as Freud discovered, is the basis of humour.

On top of this, food, like everything else in Britain, is used as a weapon in the class war. This conflict is no longer a simple confrontation between those who demand chips with everything and those who wouldn't look at a chip unless it's described as a *pomme frite*. There are now innumerable factions, unlikely alliances and many waverers. Wok-handlers and pulse-addicts are despised by well-hung meat advocates. Much depends on an ability to recognise sodium glutamate or package soup. Corner-shop reactionaries cross swords with the supermarket progressives.

All of this is reflected in these pages. Here is a feast without flatulence, a booze-up without brain damage.

LIST OF CARTOONISTS

Alan Coren

TRAVELLING HEAVY

Just the other lunchtime, in a somewhat spatchcock biscuit-coloured building on the narrow banks of the Veyle at Vonnas, a middle-aged man in a retina-wrinkling three-piece suit run up, at a guess, out of a bolt of old Black Watch curtaining, suddenly stood on his chair at the table next to mine and, after a full minute's fraught deliberation, photographed a prawn.

When he got down again, he turned to me, as if any explanation were necessary.

'Excuse me, sir,' he said. His accent betokened the Great Plains; his voice was full of family bibles and wheat. 'I hope I didn't disturb your lunch, it is just that I have always found it preferable not to go closer than four feet when photographing gourmet subjects.'

I put down a tineload of *Pigeon de Bresse en Cocotte et Foie Blond Sauté.*

'I quite understand,' I said. I have usually felt it prudent to choose civility as my best option when dealing with such people. They can be all smiles one minute, and stick an axe in your head the next.

'It is not,' he said, clearly encouraged (always a risk), 'that I do not carry a full range of auxiliary lenses, enabling me to get right down to within three inches, should the occasion demand it. I do.' Here he indicated an anodised metal suitcase beside his chair, a compact monogrammed item not much larger than the average Portakabin. 'It is simply that these introduce an unacceptable distortion factor.'

'Yes,' I said, 'they would.'

'Eat your pigeon,' said my companion.

I have never known why they are always companions, in food articles. I have never known why food writers do not come right out and lay the relationship on the line. To me, a companion always sounds like someone you got out of a small ad in *The Lady* to hold your wool and make sure your bath-chair goes for its annual service. But there you are.

I moved the shard of bird-breast towards my lips.

'Are you by any chance a photographer, sir?' said the madman.

Why do elderly Americans call people sir? Are they after a tip? I put my fork down again.

'No,' I said.

'My husband,' said the madman's wife, from across their table and through a display of flowers that, with her head in them, suggested something by Douanier Rousseau after a month or two on confiscated booze, 'has photographed every three-star menu on our trip. We are from Gary, Indiana.'

'I appreciate that,' I said.

'I have three hundred gourmet slides already,' said the husband. 'I'll be giving an illustrated talk to the Elks when I get back.'

He didn't say it with a capital E of course; I realised it had one only later. At the time, it sounded no more unreasonable than anything else.

He sat down after that, but neither of them ate much. That wasn't really why they were there, in Georges Blanc's superb restaurant *La Mère Blanc*, a few miles north of Lyon. It is one of the problems of that handful of gourmet shrines for which Michelin trot out the three rosettes: more than mere great restaurants, they are now tourist cynosures, they are cultural artefacts to be seen, snapped, souvenired and taken back to Osaka and Surbiton on Kodak slide and commemorative ashtray. And just as Chartres Cathedral is packed to the gunwales with tourists who wonder why it comes to a point instead of having a rooftop burgerbar, just as the Mona Lisa is jostled by mobs wishing to know which shutter-speed Leonardo selected, so the great hallowed eateries of France now bear the burden of customers asking for bottles of ketchup and side-orders of sauerkraut.

They are, however, well-marshalled by the steely charm of the staff and thus obtrude hardly at all upon the preoccupations of the caring gutsies who have scuttled thither for the right reasons. And, if you like food at all, there is still no better place in all the world to be, when the mouse runs up the clock, than in one of the dozen-odd spots on whose owners' stove-tanned cheeks the men from the tyre company have plonked their acclamatory kiss. It is no mere design-coincidence that the Michelin symbol is a bloke with a big belly and a somewhat glazed smile.

Indeed – since some of you may be wondering, poised as you are on the very threshold of a smart Travel Number, why I am running off, in so many senses, at the mouth when what you were reasonably expecting was a handy timetable of Bosphorus stopping-trains and the Portuguese for enterovioform – eating the best the French can bung at me has now become my only aim in travelling. I do not feel there to be a great deal of point in going anywhere else, or doing anything else when you get there. Much have I travell'd in the realms of gold, and many goodly states and kingdoms seen, the main legacy of which was the annual loss of the top level of skin and the bottom level of wallet, and few poignant memories to carry with me into life's reflective twilight. I have seen the Taj Mahal by moonlight and climbed the Great Pyramid of Giza, if that's the one on the right, I have crossed the Grand Canyon by mule, one of the most interesting acquaintances I met in Arizona, I have sweated in the Matto Grosso and cooled off in a Himalayan lake, admittedly not on the same day, I have stared at getting on for 13,000 paintings of the Madonna and Child, I have gone to the top of most things with steps, I have watched Indian television.

In thirty years, *en bref*, I have done my bit, and the remembered peaks that stick up above the fog of memory are a few French meals. Not my fault, we can't all be Patrick Leigh Fermor or Jan Morris, to take just three, what I like doing is tucking in, and henceforth I do not intend my holiday planning to go much further than M. Blanc's *Chaud-Froid de Foie Gras au Vin de Bordeaux, Bar de Ligne à la Marinière, Gratin de Homard Breton aux Huitres, Filet d'Agneau de Sisteron à la Crème de Champignons*, and *Marinade de Blanc de Poularde de Bresse Alexandre*, especially if I'm getting paid by the word.

Nor, as a matter of fact, do I now need to go much further literally. Thanks to an organisation called Le Tour Gastronomique which operates from the unlikely gustatory *endroit* of Croydon High Street, it is now possible for discerning pigs to wrap up a remarkable package: return flight to Lyon, three meals at three different cathedrals of *cuisine classique* on three different days, top hotel accommodation, a car to lug the viscera from one table to another, and all for less than £300 a mouth, all in. In other words, for half the price of ptomaine-filled fortnight on the Costa Botulisma, a man can feed on honey-dew, and drink the milk of Paradise.

Nor let it be carped that one meal a day is not enough for a growing lad. I speak as one who has grown four pounds. The joy of the chosen restaurants is that the food is so good, and goes on for so long, that not only does one need to eat nothing more for the rest of the day, one does not need to do anything more, either. Gorged into unconcern about the weather, the temperature of the pool, the availability of tennis court and local nubilia alike, one is quite happy just to stumble back to one's nest in the centre of Lyon, shower off the more persistent sauces, and doze in front of an incomprehensible telly until it is time to get up, shave, and go and have lunch again.

Wisely, the tour company has stuck its compass-point in Lyon. No city in the world is closer to more astonishing eating. On our second day, with the memory of Georges Blanc's unparalleled panwork still coming out of our pores like musk, we drove the fifty miles to Roanne and the legendary establishment of Les Frères Troisgros.

The eponymous Brothers Threefat, clearly marked from birth for a career in stuffing, have set up their stand opposite the railway station, with that occasionally irritating sans-souci with which the Frogs bang off the *grande geste*. Most of their best res-

taurants look from the outside like the kind of dumps a Berni patron wouldn't slow down for. It is possibly something to do with giving an impression of Art's priorities: remember what a sloppy dresser Van Gogh was?

I shall not dwell upon the astounding *bizarreries* that the Brothers managed to pull off that day. They do not, apart from anything else, translate well: mention Hot Gooseliver Salad and Sole Flutes, and the sensitive reader will reach for his enamel bowl, but I should be failing in my duty to a paper of record if I did not put in a stunned word for the *Homard Poché à la fondue de Tomates et Concombres*, if only to reflect upon what an incredibly long way the lobster has come since man first stubbed his toe on that ludicrous piece of Meccano sidling along the

'As you've ordered the set lunch, giving little or no consideration to our menu gastronomique, perhaps you would be good enough to remove your tie.'

sea-bed and decided, God knows how, that somewhere inside that pile of unprepossessing hinges there might be something worth eating.

Of the three restaurants visited, Threefat's was unquestionably (and engagingly) the least sacerdotal. It is essentially a local restaurant, full of bank managers with their sleeves rolled up and TVA inspectors with splashes of *sauce oursin* on their bi-focals; for the first time in my life, I heard a man at a neighbouring table, having watched his own companion mop up a third helping of duck, cry, 'Tu es une bonne fourchette!' Is there anywhere else in the world that one adult publicly congratulates another on the sheer power of his eating?

That day, we stopped lunching at four. It seemed a good idea not to overdo it. Tomorrow, there was Bocuse, and you have to be in shape.

It is not easy culturally to translate Paul Bocuse. The chef as hero is a concept that does not travel: we should have to imagine a child produced by Ian Botham and the Queen Mother who grew up to take Port Stanley single-handed and win the Nobel Peace Prize for his television chat-show, and even then we should have but a poor British equivalent of the Renaissance colossus that is Paul Bocuse.

His court is in a lay-by ten kilometres from Lyon, in a dreary cleft between the railway and the Saône. It serves the best food in the world, and it is impossible for the sensitive soul not to be humbled in the presence of each arriving plate: this man, you say, is the greatest artist the oven has ever seen, his genius has produced this wondrous thing below my bib, and all I can do with it is stick it through a hole in my face. In an hour, I could be belching Rembrandt. *Eheu fugaces*, you murmur as the truffles wink, my name is Ozymandias, cook of cooks.

'I don't know what the restaurant would do without Gaston – he whips up the most wonderfully imaginative bills.'

It slides down a treat, mind. Reverence is all well and good in its place, but after a moment or two saliva works its inexorable will and the cutlery flashes.

Soupe aux Truffes Noires, Loup en Croûte de la Méditerranée farci Mousse de Homard, Volaille de Bresse en Vessie, all come and go in the great orchestration of the gut's desire, tastes balanced and dovetailed, rhythms and reliefs counterpointed, and how are you going to break it to your tongue that it all ends tomorrow? Great cheeses melt down, *delices et gourmandises* in sweet pursuit, but he saves the best till last, he saves himself; what other *pièce de résistance* could top the meal but the mealmaker?

He shimmies from the wings, Toscanini not taking a bow so much as bestowing himself, a thick-muscled giant with an eagle's beak and a two-foot toque and the *Légion d'Honneur* around his throat, he has autographed your menu before you can stop him, he has pumped your hand, he can do ten languages, he is what the Pope could be if only he could cook, rapt Japs clap, he smiles and your spots clear up in seconds, you can play the piano again, he kisses your companion's trembling knuckle, he enquires whether you enjoyed your meal and if (his black eyes glitter) there is anything else you might conceivably want.

Like to try asking for the ketchup, Gary?

January 1983

'.. *Finally the bull becomes maddened by the sponsorship* ...'

ON THE SCENT
Merrily Harpur
catches up with gourmets abroad

'Bonjour.
Could you tell us
the way to make
rillettes de canard
aux paysannes?'

'How thrilling to be in the
very heartland of cuisine minceur!'

'I suppose that's where
Michelin got the
idea for the stars.'

'I think that garlic soup
is following us . . .'

'Oh, how delicious!
A python stuffed with a pig,
stuffed with a guinea fowl,
stuffed with apricots.'

'Now you see what comes of
drinking the local water.'

'They probably like the notes and
the coins on separate plates.'

Alan Brien

THE MADELEINE FACTOR

Food is not all eating just as sex is not all . . . well, you get the analogy. Some of my own most vivid and satisfying associations with meals have only obliquely involved the quality of the actual stuff on the table or in the bottle – even though, of course, this was where the synaptic circuit had been initiated and completed. Thus I shall never forget the sight of my bullet-headed brother, Eric, then an obstinate seventeen, wearing one Sunday noon a sort of melting coronet of turnip slivers, potato beads and mutton fronds which my father had just tipped from a plate on to his crop-haired skull.

When I was a boy in Sunderland, youngest of a large family, we usually finished Sunday dinner by one p.m. In those days I never thought much about the menu – a word I did not know, and even now find hard to pronounce. I concentrated on stuffing myself, boa-constrictor style, with as large a boulder of sustenance as would last me out, despite hunger pains, through afternoon fantasy games among my friends, until the next obligatory Sabbatarian intake on our council estate, tea. (Never, anyway where we lived, known as *high* tea.)

Spooling back the memory reels on the old cauliflower tape-recorder, I detect a certain undulant variation in our weekly meal that I overlooked then. I knew we did not eat the same things every time, naturally. But it did not occur to me that there was any reason for that other than the well-known, unpredictable shiftiness of all adults, a deviant species incapable of perceiving that nothing

could be better than fish and chips, followed by ice-cream, any day.

But I see now that our peak must have been roast beef and Yorkshire pudding. Otherwise why, like many ageing gluttons, do I continue to stampede before me all other cooks, amateur and professional, demanding to know why my mother (lately departed at the age of 96 for the great kitchen range in the sky) could regularly produce such soft, weeping-pink ovals of meat, encircled by dark, crisp bark edged with beige fat, from her slow, unresponsive oven and her cheapest cut, which Simpson's only rarely succeeds in duplicating and few other restaurants even understand should be their ambition?

Such a treat, my hindsight saga goes on, would have been the climax of the sort of week when my father, senior fitter at the municipal tram-sheds, had been working a lot of overtime and my mother had managed to relocate some interest on our running debts. The next step-down might be a shoulder of lamb (not just a word – in those days a sharp divide lay between junior and senior sheep, on the hook as on the hoof). This would linger long at low heat until each moist morsel, under a delicate, transparent armour of fat, slid of its own accord from the sculptured bones on to the serving platter.

More frequent would be a dish in which the scarcity of the protein was counter-balanced by the generosity of the carbohydrate signalling a short week at work. The meat contribution was either steak and kidney pieces or mutton chop. Neither was quite the superior ingredient, in price or looks, that the name might suggest. The steak and kidney (I remember because I would have to wait until the butcher's closing time to collect them) consisted of curled chips and ragged blobs left over from richer orders and bore the same relation to the heavy haunches from which they came as a pile of sawdust to a fallen forest giant. The chops only too nearly resembled their name. They were small crosses or long sticks of bone, meagrely dressed with rags of flesh, as if the result of an attack on an old ram by a blind, mad assassin wielding an axe.

It was simply their looks that put off the choosier customer and relegated them to our price range. The taste was hardly a whit impaired, if at all. The steak and kidney fragments, thickened with gravy powder, became a molten, chocolatey mass packaged within a suet casing like an inverted policeman's helmet. The surface would be flaky, biscuity, with a Hollywood tan except where an occasional dark gooey gusher broke through and dyed the crust. Inside, the pastry was nearer new dough, a kind of pale lava, embedded with meaty bits like precious stones in a seam.

The suet which accompanied the mad axeman's gobbets was formed into dumplings and simmered below the surface along with the meat and veg. This too was a delicious dish on the palate though it is difficult to make it sound so in words – pale-grey or fish-belly white most of its ingredients, the juice green and watery, the dumplings themselves balls of wallpaper paste.

'The hungry man has no eyes in his belly,' runs the old Russian proverb. No, it doesn't, but it's still true even though I just made it up. In fact, *everything* my mother cooked was delicious. Far from wanting to complain about our diet in the depths of the pre-war Depression, I must confess that, though a trifle starved between meals, I never ate so well afterwards as I did during those innocent, free-range, organically-grown, chemical-free days long ago.

The hierarchy of Sunday dinners I have erected applies only to cost and not at all to taste. But there was one that we all thought just a tiny bit inferior – an Irish stew, *without* dumplings or potatoes, basically bones and beans, which tended to be served in emergencies. (It goes without saying that in the pre-war, working-class North-East only mass slaughter across the entire estate would have been considered a reasonable excuse for any self-respecting household to gather round a non-hot meal as Sunday dinner.) And it was this that my father had prepared that memorable day, my mother being in hospital, when brother Eric refused to accept this low-grade substitute.

My father was the handiest of handymen.

'The haute cuisine isn't what it used to be.'

Any technical task performed in front of him he could reproduce instantly. He re-wired the electricity, renovated the plumbing, painted and wallpapered, laid carpet and lino, grew fruit and roses. He soled all our shoes and cut all our hair. Naturally, he could cook and had several times, during mother's absence, conjured up tremendous Christmas dinners with all the trimmings. All he asked (a trait I have inherited) was afterwards to be told – 'You're marvellous!' It need only be said once. It need not be sincerely meant or even sound sincerely meant. He just liked to hear it. And nobody was in any doubt he deserved to be indulged.

On this occasion, my brother Eric – 'the German' we called him because of his Prussian implacability – refused the formula. Indeed, he volunteered the view the food was un-eatable as far as he was concerned. And as we all watched, and we could not

have been more gripped as bystanders at an assassination, the tilted helping slowly slid, defying gravity, atom by atom, on to the defiant bonce.

Since then, I have always regarded Sunday dinner as a sacred ceremony. I kept my children at it until, as teenagers, they kept bunking off for the day, wanting to eat this weekend early, that weekend late. There was an awful period when I fell in with the wrong set and often didn't eat Sunday dinner *at all*! But for the last few years, I have re-instituted the ritual. Not every weekend, but say one in three, and basically for neighbouring friends, and floating offspring. (They've become keener now they've had experience of how expensive it is to pay for your own grub.) Nobody these days will risk suet, and either beef has changed or I haven't got the knack, so I stick to slow roasting, with rosemary and honey, of shoulders of lamb.

They always seem to go down well, aided by my wife's mounds of garlic peas and golden bombs of roast potato. NW5 has lots of Greek butchers, and they are people who seem to possess an affinity with sheep (at least when dead) so the meat is always first-class. I can't say I remember much about the actual food myself, being busy cutting up everybody's portion and feeding them with a spoon. But I have introduced one improvement from Sunderland days – wine. Then, we had to pretend that we did not know where the pub was, owing to my mother's teetotalism. Now, I pour away like the many-armed goddess Kali.

And to make sure all will be well – 'You're marvellous!' they shout – I begin and end, as I prefer most things in life to begin and end, with a large Scotch whisky. Serenely sure, the epicure can say, Fate cannot harm me, I have whiskied today.

'I want something completely expressionless.'

July 1986

Glynn Christian's

SURREAL CHEESE GUIDE

Last year I sat at a ceremonious London banquet for some *confrérie* or other for French cheese. The table was a mixed board of ten varieties of local cheese, food and magazine people. When our cheese came it was a good, simple selection, which had responsibly been kept cool until the last moment. Just as I was about to make some suitable congratulatory remark, a very famous British food photographer with Frenchy pretensions hissed across the table at his partner: '*Pas le Stilton, darling, c'est refrigeré.*'

This grisly public display of low taste demonstrates the battle true cheese-lovers fight against posturing: like red wine, banquet cheese is far better served cool than at the usual sweat. And safer, too.

Somewhere, I suppose, there's a name for people like that photographer; well, Peter York will have one, if that counts. They swank and smirk if they serve cheese before pudding, are positively puffed with their array of exclamations of recognition, and fair burst to be first to identify what is laid before them. I love to watch them, hate to listen to them and giggle at the sheer greed which forces them to plunge a knife into anything which once was milk. Experimental and creative dining is one thing, but there's nothing like a cheese-board to expose how few diners really care about or know what they are eating.

I blame the insidious modern belief that anything traditional, any food remotely connected with the past, or with peasants, or

with both, is better if not best. Certainly we need reminding of the pleasures of simple foods simply prepared. But blindly eating rural French cheeses which are visibly glowing in puddles of their own perspiring decay in smarty-pants British restaurants is nothing to do with that. Very few are anything like the originals; if they were, none of us would make it to the pudding. Even if they were traditional, and in an acceptable condition, the next best guarantee of an upset stomach is to eat cheese of any sort which has been left exposed to the air at room temperature. Air and warmth rot cut cheese faster than it ripens.

I suppose you could argue that by eating rustic, little recognised cheeses, you're helping the peasants improve their life-style, putting them on an upward social learning curve and so on. Ha ha. They're grateful all right; they've been trying to get off the stuff for centuries and to live on real food. For heaven's sake, why did millions of peasants up clogs and take to the streets of America? To die happy with a mouthful of processed Kraft, that's why. We have conveniently forgotten that most eaters of traditional foods did so, not through choice, but because, like food mountains, they were there. Heaven help the Lyonnais aesthete who didn't like putrid lumps of last year's milk smelling like open-air lavs in August ... Eat it up, Jean-Luc-Marie-Tracé, or starve. I don't expect you hear that said a lot at the Waterside Inn.

Traditional country-dwellers had the benefit neither of Rural-Living part-works, nor of a Women's Institute to teach peasant mums a different sort of cheese, nor of pooh-poohing food critics telling them their goats were the wrong variety or that cheese-life was better in the next valley. Now there are such things, the journalists eat peasant food and *they* use the money to eat real food at last, from packets.

You know what I'd like to do to them, don't you? No, not the peasants, those cheese-board Charlies. I'd like to make up a really disgusting 'traditional' cheese-board, cut a piece out of each cheese, leave them by the central heating under a cheese-bell, which will be removed from time to time to let in cigarette smoke and flambé fumes and so people might cough at them in passing, you know, the way a restaurant would, then serve those cheeses amidst a really terrifically good meal with beautiful wines. It's usually called contrast: it would actually be revenge.

For something French and rural I would have had to marry an auvergnat maid. As part of her dowry she would bring *gaperons*, and plenty of them. Indeed, our bosoms would only have cloven one to the other because she was well-hung, by which I mean that *gaperons* are hemispheres of cheese made from skimmed milk, garlic and black pepper. Traditionally, a father with a marriageable daughter would hang such cheeses outside the house where they grew exceptional beards of arresting length and colour as they matured. The more displayed, the more marriageable the girls, although I suppose there might come the stage when a real dog of a daughter offered more upstairs than down. That's been known.

I would offer much more, upstairs and downstairs, to ensure eating less or none of a hairy *gaperon* or of the next two cheeses, the filthy *crottin de diable* or devil's droppings and *fromage fort*.

Like most horrible cheeses, *crottins* start off perfectly nicely, made with creamy goat's milk in Sancerre. They are protected with an AOC, like wines, and early in spring are rich and delicious. As summer progresses they get stronger, and some are kept over winter, going brown and rank and becoming *crottins*, in fact a dead common word for horse droppings. If the cheese board Charlies managed to eat even that, a *fromage fort* from Burgundy would gingerly be unlidded. For this excrescence you must first allow little cheeses of the *crottin* persuasion

to go right off. Something like the appalling dark brown buttons of *chevreton de Macon*, which get right up your nose at a hundred paces. You mix them with a little butter, perhaps some leek water, certainly some *marc de Bourgogne* but not your best, and a few herbs. This is sealed and left for several months and from time to time you stir back in such hideous moulds and growths as erupt: a distasteful but important step. If you don't, the compound is likely to explode.

Oh, and in case this is still too subtle for your pure, unsullied, clean, green, peasant palate, it is served with garlic and onion. Lovely after a little fish with a banana and caper sauce, for instance, as both would be triumphs of technique and necessity over taste; and in this I suppose you can see how ghastly little cheeses have managed to insinuate themselves into *nouvelle*-ish meals, where the plate is ever more important than the palate.

I probably wouldn't be able to find for my selection any of the cheeses made with Mongolian mare's milk (oh, yes they do) but I would manage some of our very own ancient British cheeses. Some Blue Vinney, made with skimmed milk and clouded rather than veined with blue; it was famed for toughness rather than flavour, which is why fromophiles (is that the word for them?) who have never tasted it go on about how good it was. Rubbish. Same goes for most old British cheeses. The cream went to the big houses and only skimmed milk went to make pressed cheeses for the serfs' 'white meat'. Suffolk cheese was hard and dry, and Pepys's staff complained if they were given it. Thin, miserable people were called Banbury cheeses. Hard British cheeses were the pitiful last resort of the starving or the mean, and hence the expression 'hard cheese'.

And I would add an early Stilton. It would be unpasteurised, oh bliss, hand-wrought, and delivered directly by those sweet Leicestershire milkmaids via the Bell Inn at

Stilton by coach down the Great North Road. But only if they were well enough. Until pasteurisation, most milkmaids contracted tuberculosis or brucellosis like anything, and were pink-cheeked only because of this, very rude health I call that. Naturally, the Stilton would be sliced rather than scooped, for that is a dreadfully *nouveau* thing to do. Yet there would still be a scoop in attendance; the traditional implement for scraping up the writhing infestation of cheese mites which always enrobed a decent Stilton. Eat them up, I would say, they are traditional. And the fromophiles probably would.

I wonder if such a cheese-board would really teach my enthusiasts to appreciate a single, perfectly presented and recognisable modern cheese, even if a little *refrigeré*? In case it wouldn't, I'd also offer what I consider the Mr and Mrs of horrible cheeses.

Fromage de monsieur is actually a rather nice, creamy, Brie-type modern cheese. But I would ever so quietly remind my fromophiles, in their mid-mouth ecstasy, that its name is what bilingual schoolboys, with accurate olfactory recall, christen the penial produce of the uncircumcised. What a wheeze it would be as they retched. But it would only be a wheeze, a joke. So we would move on to a thirteenth-century ancestor of *cendre de champagne*. They would smack their lips and roll their eyes and I would agree it's wonderful, marvellous, and *really* traditional. This cheese is now aged in ashes but, according to ancient custom, it used to be matured under the bed in a pool of *urine feminine*; it was known about the banks of Châlons-sur-Marne as *fromage de cul*. A lovely wee cheese, I would say with sincerity.

July 1986

Head Waiter (the Old Gent had wished for a stronger Cheese). "HI! JAMES—LET LOOSE THE GORGONZOLA!"

David Taylor

THOSE DISTURBING ADDITIVES

Philip Hood

Just what's in today's tasty treats? Can it make you shake? In tests, four out of five laboratory mice lost all track of time when force-fed convenience foods. Two out of three came up in funny blotches and one in nine fell over. Many doctors more or less agree that chemicals can perhaps under certain conditions in some people but not all the time contribute to 'tummy ache' or shrieking for no good reason. But the industrial food giants say dopey housewives will not buy bland, unappetising, tired-looking things that smell and might be off. Probably millions eat only artificial foods and seem to be right as rain.

Now caring people are concerned.

We sent plain-cover consumers out into the supermarkets to buy disgusting muck and subjected it to stringent tests. The report makes disturbing reading for anyone concerned about today's aware eating, the poisoned larder, threatened species or health and safety in the kitchen.

In the first of 200 weekly extracts, we list in full what goes into a typical Euro-pastie.

● A 12-minute audio-visual aid, *You Would Not Credit It*, is available mail-order from The European Gunk Inspectorate, Tartrazine House, Riboflavinstraße, Brussels W1A 1AA

KNOW YOUR E-NUMBERS

E638 Emulsified pig's spleen extract (strawberry)

E639 Emulsified pig's spleen extract (cheese & onion)

E640 Conglomerated sheepshank

E641 Permitted gum

E642 Another permitted gum

E643 Complex fatty arbuckles (*NOT Belgium*)

E643 (a) Belgian caramelised marmoset gumbo particles

E644 Circumspect (synthetic herb)

E645 Butylated orthophosphoric benzoate (crispy bacon)

E646 Water-based plumping agent
E647 Bovine umbilical suilage
E647 (a) Brilliant green
E647 (b) Half-japanned goose rosin (raspberry)
E648 Synthetic bacterial stiffener (Mom's recipe)
E648 (a) Clotted eel
E648 (b) Clarified dogfish liver spume
E649 Intimidated pectin
E650 Uncracked Soviet marine diesel residue (prawn)
E651 Bulker
E652 Ethyl 4-hydroxybenzoate methyl slurry (oven-fresh)
E653 Fulmeric nitrate (boil-in-the-bag)

E654 Fulmeric nitrate (just pop under the grill)
E655 Fulmeric nitrate (stir'n'serve)
E656 Fulmeric nitrate (for the way we live today)
E657 Fulmeric nitrate (Cap'n Tastebud)
E658 Yellow
E659 Artificial yellow gumbo spores
E660 G-Glucono disodium ribonucleotide lactylate (folioles)
E661 Slug-based coagulant (country style)
E662 Slug-based coagulant (gooseberry surprise)
E663 Slug-based coagulant (kosher)
E664 Country-style gooseberry concentrate (slug pellets)

'Ah! Canned asparagus spears, like my mother used to open.'

E665 Boiled animal extract on a stick

E666 Myrmecophilous sodium alginate syrup (smooth)

E667 Myrmecophilous sodium alginate syrup (creamy)

E668 Ethyl ester of beta-apo-8'-lycopene (C_{31}) (breast)

E669 Ethyl ester of beta-apo-8'-lycopene (C_{31}) (leg)

E670 Ethyl ester of beta-apo-8'-lycopene (C_{31}) (portion)

E671 Poly-putta-ketalon

E672 Hydroxypropylmethylcellulose (standard)

E673 Hydroxypropylmethylcellulose (metallic)

E674 Cocoa cultures

E675 Carbonated hen waste

E676 Fermented hen waste

E677 Artificial barbecued curd

E678 Hoof sludge glutamate (thousand island)

E678 (a) Diabetic sucroglyceride monopalminate (farm fresh)

E679 Edible sausage knotting

E680 Lactylated savoury beeswax (Cornish)

E681 Dark brown

E682 Simulated beetroot

E683 Protoplasmic tongue lubricant

E684 Slubbing agent

E685 Permitted pulper

E686 *mono*Potassium L − (+)edible feldspar (spring onion)

E687 Nucleolo-centrosome nicotonic kipper stain (gloss)

E688 Nucleolo-centrosome nicotonic kipper stain (matt)

E689 Nucleolo-centrosome nicotonic kipper (eggshell)

E690 Benzene rings

E691 Benzylated onion rings

E692 Partially smelted cingulum (bone-based)

E693 Differential custard

E694 Certain ventricles

E695 Follicular metatartaric whey

E696 Castellated ox filaments

E697 Epicranial veal slime

E697 (a) Moderated skunk

E698 Radical masticatory amalgam

E699 Monolithic spigoted sardine substitute

E700 Skulker

E701 Adulterated goose pimples (cuboid)

E702 Suffocated peach halves (*except* Luxembourg)

E703 Bright orange dye

E704 Potassium guttersnipe

E705 Sympathy (paste)

E706 Disjointed loosening agent

E707 Scissile mollusc concentrate

E708 Limpet wax

E709 Edible head waste (cuppa noodles)

E710 Serried barnacle eyelets

E711 Comminuted pig's withy

E712 Aggravated blue

E713 Participating ossicles

E714 Vulcanised locust adipocere

E715 Furfuraceous nutmeg

E716 Immutable ghee

E717 Eviscerated marmot flavouring

E718 Agitated *di*-calcium diorthophosphate (spam)

E719 Yacht varnish

E720 Unidentified frying object (tests continue)

'It's not the way mother used to heat fish-fingers!'

March 1986

'It's the only way I can get him to eat anything.'

Ralph Schoenstein

FOOD LIKE MOTHER USED TO CHUCK OUT

Yesterday morning, while merrily eating a green pea sandwich, I began to wonder if there was a phrase to describe the opposite of haute cuisine. Would it be naught cuisine? Well, whatever it is, I have spent my life enjoying it, for a curious flaw in my palate – I guess you could call it bad taste – has made me a traveller in the culinary underworld.

The first misplaced salivation that I can recall occurred at the age of six, when my father took me to a baseball game and bought me a hot dog, thus dramatically introducing me to the world of third-rate food.

'I'm afraid that these ballpark hot dogs aren't very good,' my father said.

'Oh, I *love* them,' I said and then asked for another.

The following week at a delicatessen, I tried a legitimate frankfurter and hated it. What I had liked at the ballpark was a kind of meaty neutrality, a frankfurter from which the flavour had been lovingly removed, a dish that existed only to keep the mustard off the roll.

Of course, I probably wouldn't have minded just some mustard on a roll because I soon found myself enjoying the dubious delights of mayonnaise sandwiches. I invented this off-beat delicacy one day after my mother had made a sandwich of bologna and mayonnaise for me. The initial bite informed me that I couldn't enjoy the bologna because it had a clearly defined taste, like a good frankfurter; so I removed it and carried on with just the bread and mayonnaise. In fact, in a moment that bordered on cosmic insight, I wondered how many other sandwich eaters secretly preferred the mayonnaise to the meat but went along with the latter as a sop to society.

From that day on, my dejected mother would often hear me cry, 'Make me a sandwich, Mom. Hold the meat.'

My mother did what she could to discourage my adventures in tastelessness, but she was working against my grandmother who was an inspiration to me, mostly by making matzo balls that never quite came off. Whenever someone talks to me about food that is like the kind that grandmother used to make, he is talking about the reason that my grandfather often ate out. A charmingly free spirit, my grandmother didn't like being locked into recipes: she cooked by ear, but she was gastronomically tone deaf. She had, however, an appreciative guest in me, for I grew to love the uncertain treat of eating her matzo balls, which were sometimes too hard and sometimes too soft but always neutral in taste. Only once did I find myself dipping them in mayonnaise.

'The boy just likes bland food,' my father said to my mother in a seminar about my mouth. 'We just can't take him to Mexico.'

'We can't even take him to Canada,' my mother said.

Not only did I lean towards food that was bland but towards food that was soft as well, for chewing was my least favourite form of exercise. It was, therefore, just a matter of time before I discovered creamed corn, which I soon was eating directly from the can because I like my neutral dishes to be served at room temperature. My parents, of course, cringed whenever they saw me sucking in a whole can of corn. It was the ideal dish for someone who had just lost a heavyweight fight, but not for a boy of twelve whose teeth were turning into souvenirs.

One day my father and I were about to go out together. He came into the kitchen, looked with dismay at my favourite snack, and said, 'Hurry up and drink your corn.'

Throughout public school and college, I stayed with my old standbys: meatless hot dogs and mayonnaise sandwiches sometimes dunked in corn. When I was twenty-one, however, I entered the Army and made another great leap forward by discovering chipped beef on toast, which had an alternate name that involved some roofing material. This particular dish, given to soldiers to toughen them for battle, was an acquired taste; but I was perhaps the only man to ever have acquired it. The ingredients were nonchoice hunks of beef, soggy toast, and nondescript cream sauce. In combination, however, they took their place beside something that my grandmother could have made at a ballpark.

A few years after leaving the Army, I got married, fathered a baby girl, and found a whole new world of drinkable food. I fed Jill whenever I could, sometimes gaily at 3.00 a.m., so I could share her mashed bananas, mashed carrots, and mashed pears. Baby food, of course, did contain some delicious tastes, but the total lack of things to chew more than made up for this flaw. Jill's meals let me relive my golden boyhood days with liquid corn.

Four years later, my wife had a second child, no doubt to end the embarrassment of having visitors catch me eating baby food alone. Her name was Eve-Lynn and we shared some precious moments slurping apricots and prunes. But then, like Jill, she deserted me for goulash and seeded rye.

Eve-Lynn had just turned six when I decided that the time had come for me to blaze another trail through the land of naught cuisine. And so, one afternoon, in a burst of gastronomic creativity, I put some baby green peas between two slices of soft white bread and the green pea sandwich was born.

My daughters were both ecstatic.

'My father eats green pea sandwiches!' Jill announced to the neighbourhood, while my wife began looking at real estate ads.

To prove that this inspired snack was no mere accident, I quickly returned to the drawing board and the spaghetti-on-white appeared, which so delighted Eve-Lynn that she sat right down and invented the mustard-on-white herself. I had to take a little credit for that one, of course, because the daughter of the mayonnaise sandwich king certainly had the seeds of the mustard sandwich in her genes.

A few weeks ago, Jill entered her teens at a party where she happily ate spicy ham, curried chicken, and Camembert cheese.

'I'm sorry, Dad,' she said with a mouth full of garlic dill pickle.

'That's okay, darling,' I told her. 'The lover of neutral food often walks a lonely road.'

And then I went off to visit a friend in a hospital, where I finished a meal by his bed that he said was too awful to eat, a meal whose highlight was a gelatinous blob that was either custard, pudding, or something else. There's nothing that gives me the cheer of a good institutional meal, just like the kind that my grandmother used to make.

July 1975

'Sorry, sir, we're closed. The speciality of the house just ran off with the head-waiter.'

Miles Kington

I'M THE CHEF OF ARABY

A catering firm has won a £1 million contract – to supply sandwiches to the Arabs...

K Snacks of Wolverhampton is to ship an initial 45,000 chicken, beef and cheese sandwiches to Qatar.

The sandwiches will be sent in what the firm describes as 'a refrigerated form. They will be chilled in Wolverhampton and the sandwiches will be around two days old when they arrive in the Persian Gulf,' said a spokesman.

The spokesman added: 'The contract at present will last us for nine months. It is a fantastic order – it really is unbelievable. It will transform us from a small firm to a large and prosperous one.'

– Daily Telegraph.

From Frank Wrigley
Manager, Sam's Sandwiches
Birmingham
    Dear Sheik Qemar al Azrami,
I note receipt of your inquiry re our take-away and office lunch supply service. I therefore enclose a copy of our Express Midday Super Service sales sheet, and hope it will be of interest to your Department of Nutrition in Muscat.

Please note that several lines are now withdrawn, notably Pork, Pork and Gherkin, Pork and Salad, and Toasted Bacon.

Looking forward to your esteemed order,
    I remain

From the Manager
To the Production Manager
    Ron, this could be our lucky day! Our first Arab customer, no less. A Sheik from Muscat, presumably coming over here for a big exhibition in Birmingham or some such. Maybe he's here to have a look at Birmingham City's next home game, with a view to buying Alf Ramsey for the Muscat Ramblers, who knows?

How many extra sandwiches could we produce at short notice? 50? 100 even? Let me know.

Not much demand for the new corn beef'n'alfalfa sprout on rye, I'm afraid. Can we have a rethink on this one?

To Sheik Qemar al Azrami
    Dear Sheik,
    I thank you for your sample order received this morning, but feel there must be some clerical error, as the number of chicken sandwiches you quote is 1,000, repeat, 1,000, and ditto for beef, cheese and peanut butter. Could you please at your leisure state correct figure required for each flavour, which I presume is not correct.

In response to your detailed inquiries as to other tasty snack fillings: cress is a small, vitamin-rich herb eaten raw in England: cottage cheese is a smooth, mild white mixture: so, for that matter, is mayonnaise, salad cream and margarine.

I can particularly recommend the corn beef'n'alfalfa sprouts, a new filling which we are pioneering and for which there is much demand.

Awaiting your corrected order,
    I remain

To the Production Director
    Sorry, Ron, old son – false alarm about the rich Arab, I think. Some nutter who thinks we can send a boy on a motorbike round downtown Muscat with 4,000 rounds every day. I appreciate you could lay on 100 extra, but can't see Terry on his Yamaha leaving here at 11 am and getting to Muscat by lunch-time, even the way he rides. I know that our slogan is 'Sandwiches Supplied, Any Place, Any Time', but surely any fool knows that *Any Place* means *in the Birmingham area*, and not too far out even then? I mean, who'd want to supply Wolverhampton, for heaven's sake?

Now it's October, might as well give the tuna'n'cucumber a miss till next year.

To Sheik Qemar al Azrami
    Honoured Sheik,
I welcome the prompt reply to my doubts about your numerical error. I note that there was indeed a clerical error, and that when you asked a quote for 1,000 rounds each of four fillings, the figure 1,000 was incorrect. The figure should have been 10,000. Repeat, 10,000.

Our estimate for this important order will be given priority treatment and should reach Muscat almost immediately.

I note your inquiry as to whether pork is used in our liver sausage, pate and salami sandwiches. I confirm, as requested by the beard of the prophet, that no trace of the unclean animal is involved.

To the Production Director

Ron, before you read the next paragraph, I would like you to take a stiff drink, sit down and relax. No, seriously, OK, ready?

How soon can you undertake to produce an extra order of 40,000 rounds, a quarter of beef, cheese, chicken and peanut butter? Every day?

Calm down, Ron. Be your age. Think what it means. This Arab is serious. He writes on official Muscat paper. Behind him is the fabulous wealth of the oil of the East, unimaginable fortunes which can grant every whim known to man. In his case, his whim is to order 40,000 rounds of English sarnies. You know and I know that the object in question is white and unappealing, and that in a man-to-man talk we might advise him to settle for something more exotic. Like fish and chips, or hamburgers.

But may I also point out that this could make our fortune? Get us an Export Award or two? And help to pay an outstanding bill or two, notably for your order of alfalfa sprouts?

PS. Can you confirm that we use no pork in our liver sausage, pate or salami sandwiches?

PPS. I will, of course, put our Sheik friend off as much as possible until we are ready to supply his order.

To Sheik Qemar al Azrami
Esteemed Sheik,
May I inquire whether you wish the order to be on white or on brown?
I remain

To Production Director

I don't care. Buy a chicken farm. Write to President Carter for the peanut butter. Rustle as many cattle as you need. But *do* something. Of course it's possible! It just means hiring a few more people, getting a new place and setting up a new system, that's all. And buying a bakery, of course. I'd do it myself if I wasn't so busy costing the whole thing.

I do not consider your suggestion of hiring Concorde helpful.

To Sheik Qemar al Azrami
O Sheik
I confirm your wish that the sandwiches should be on brown. May I take this opportunity of inquiring whether you wish salt with the chicken, mustard with the beef or pickles with the cheese? All these extras are, needless to say, free.
I remain

To Production Director

I herewith return your resignation. I have committed myself to producing a costed quotation for the Sheik and cannot put him off much longer. The only thing I have not asked him so far is whether he wants paper napkins. I have just had a snotty letter from the Sheik saying that offering extras free is bad business, and that he insists on paying for them. Please let me have full plans for production by tomorrow morning.

I have reconsidered your suggestion for Concorde. I think it is a good one. With a bit of luck, it will get the sandwiches there before they curl up.

To Sheik Qemar al Azrami
O mighty Sheik
I have broken down the cost of supplying 40,001 sandwiches to you daily (the extra one being the sample corn beef'n'alfalfa you have requested) as follows:–

To making 40,001 sandwiches @ 25p each	£10,000 25p
To packing and wrapping @ 10p each	£ 4,000 10p
Transport to Heathrow	£ 200
Flight to Muscat via Bahrein	£ 3,500
Extras (salt, mustard etc)	£ 2,000 02p
40,000 paper napkins	£ 3,000
Helpful payments to customs men, etc	£ 5,500
Total	£28,200 52p
Service charge of 12%	£ 3,300 48p
	£31,500
VAT @ 8%	£ 2,520
Total	£34,020

I remain

To Production Director

Ron, would you stop sending me your resignation? Not only does it create extra paperwork to send it back, it is also not very good for staff morale. Ta.

You will be pleased to hear that there is very little likelihood of having to send sandwiches to the Middle East. After I have costed it out, the daily shipment would set our Arab friend back about £34,000 a day, or nearly £1 per sandwich. Not even an Arab would stomach that. I fancied the idea of throwing in a Coke as well and charging £1.50 per sandwich, but there are limits. Well, aren't there?

Oh well, it was a nice dream while it lasted.

To Sheik Qemar al Azrami
   Sheik of Sheiks,
I acknowledge receipt of your letter of the 27th and note the contents.
               I remain

To Production Director
   Bad news I'm afraid, Ron. As I predicted, the Sheik does not accept our estimate of £34,000 daily for sandwiches to Muscat. What I failed to predict was that he found this an awkward figure and would prefer to make it a round £40,000.
   We are now committed to producing sandwiches for the Arab market at £1 a throw. I would welcome a detailed breakdown from you on how we shall achieve this. I would be grateful if it did not involve your resignation.

To Sheik Qemar al Azrami
   O Sheik of Sheik of Sheiks,
I hereby contract to undertake the supply of 40,000 sandwiches daily, as agreed per letter.
               I remain

To Production Director
   Thank you for your long, powerful, though somewhat emotional memo, Ron. I agree with your following points.
 – That we have not built up a small, happy, city lunch-time firm in order to involve ourselves in a big international cartel and bring on ourselves the kind of ulcer-laden worries so well described in the *Sunday Times* series on Mr Onassis.
 – That our only hope of sure survival is to apply for an Arts Council Grant or massive loan.
 – That by supplying a huge daily airlift to the Middle East, we will run the danger of losing the personal touch whereby we can phone a client to say: 'Sorry, pate's off, will liver sausage be all right?'
 – That by becoming a big company we will only lose ourselves in the depths of government bureaucracy and soullessness.
 – That small is beautiful, big is ugly and that we should adopt the course of action you recommend.

From the Official Receiver
To Sheik Qemar al Azrami
   Dear Sheik,
I am sorry to inform you that Sam's Sandwiches of Birmingham have gone into voluntary liquidation. Although he asked me not to inform anyone, I feel obliged to tell you that Mr Frank Wrigley is now trading under the name of Brum Take-Away Kebabs, to whom any further correspondence should be addressed.
   I am sorry you did not like the corn beef'n'alfalfa sandwich. Your account has been credited to the extent of 25p.
           yours faithfully

October 1977

Kenneth Tynan

A NIGHT AT THE OMAR KHAYYAM

The Omar Khayyam Hotel in Cairo, after a short stay in which I am now convalescent, is a converted palace that was built to house the Empress Eugénie when she visited Egypt in 1869 for the opening of the Suez Canal. Whether it has in fact been converted into a *hotel* is the subject I want to discuss. It certainly looks as a hotel ought to look – i.e. like a palace built to house the Empress Eugénie in 1869. It has numbers on the doors and a reception desk and a rapacious concierge and it charges (a great deal) for the use of its rooms. But it does not, as I shall soon demonstrate, *behave* like a hotel. My own theory, based on deduction and hunch, is that since being nationalised by the government of the United Arab Republic, it has been converted from a converted palace into a rehabilitation centre for backsliders who still yearn for a privileged way of life – a sort of crazy house for unreformed bourgeois sympathisers. It operates, I believe, on the behaviourist principle of aversion therapy. 'If this is the splendour you long for,' it implies, 'you must be out of your unreconstructed mind.'

I say 'implies' because the message steals up on you with great subtlety. Nobody clubs you over the head and tells you to go back to work on the High Dam. Let me describe how the process works. My wife and I began our two-day visit by dining in the 'hotel' restaurant. An ashtray no bigger than a man's hand was placed on the table before us. On it were written the words: 'Shepheard's Hotel.' This, the first hint that all was not well, provoked the first tremor of displacement.

My wife then ordered pea soup from the *table d'hôte*. Bright red tomato soup was instantly and enthusiastically poured out for her. The concept of serving the wrong thing with the right efficiency proved to be typical of the 'hotel's' approach to its job. Instead of the advertised *poulet en cocotte*, my wife was proudly given a little grey steak. (*Médaillon de chameau*, perhaps). When she made an enquiry, she was told there was no more chicken, but it was not explained why the only alternative should be a little grey steak, nor why no warning had been given of the change.

Meanwhile I had looked at the wine list and been enraptured. Among its clarets were an Haut Brion '45, a Lafite '42 and a Mouton/Rothschild '49, all at less than the equivalent of £3 a bottle: dirt cheap by English standards. Salivating at the prospect of such a bargain, I ordered Haut Brion. Fifteen minutes later the waiter told me there was none left. A pity, I felt; but no matter; the Lafite – of a year with which I was unfamiliar – might well be an even more exciting choice. The waiter grinned knowingly and left. Ten minutes later he was back: the Lafite too was finished. It was the work of not much more than half an hour to establish that not one of the 17 clarets on the list still existed in the cellar. Having made this report, the waiter withdrew, but he seemed to have been moved by my dismay, for he soon reappeared with a bottle of Burgundy, labelled 'Volnay-Santenots 1945,' which did not figure on the wine list. Would I like to try it? It was ominously ullaged, but its credentials looked very promising, so I said yes.

What followed was a classic example of Khayyam therapy. At the first touch of the corkscrew, before any pressure had been applied, the cork disintegrated completely and crumbled into the wine. The waiter immediately poured the taste through a tea-strainer *which he already had in his pocket*. If you have never tasted cork-sprinkled wine from an Egyptian cellar (or boiler-room, to judge from its condition) served through a tea-strainer, you do not know what it is like to drink warm Ribena mixed with rock salt and ammonia. The experience had, of course, the intended effect of making me wonder why I had ever liked wine. Shaking my head (and, more jovially, my fist), I sent the bottle back. The waiter nodded and said he was sure I would enjoy some proper Egyptian wine more. 'Egyptian wine,' he said with the air of a kindly man educating halfwits, 'is *fresh*.' The technique behind this whole episode was flawless. First, the promise of great treats, which are dangled and then removed. Next, the promise of an

unscheduled treat, a special privilege. Finally, the revelation that the special treat is a peculiarly revolting penalty. Hitchcock himself could not have played on one's nerves with more inventive sadism.

My main dish was an extremely virulent but none the less palatable curry. I wondered how this could have happened. Was some saboteur at large in the kitchen, preparing edible dishes in bold defiance of official policy? I learned the answer an hour or so later, when my wife and I had gone up to our room. The lavatory, of which by then I stood in some need, did not work. The edibility of the curry was no more an accident than its virulence. No sooner had I realised this than my wife made two other discover-

'*Don't touch the kebabs.*'

ies. There was no hot water in the wash-basin, and none in the bath. 'So much for your filthy revisionist whims!' I imagined the head of the Gyppu (the Cairo Security Police) sneering as he peered at us through a spyhole in the fake Gobelin tapestry. The bedroom was vast, genuinely palatial in aspect and set about with ornate standard lamps; but shaving, hot baths and the flushing of the toilet were precluded. I sourly reflected that package tourists from Uzbekhistan (of whom there had been dozens in the restaurant) would probably be too overwhelmed by the mere sight of *taps* to be upset when no hot water emerged – even from the cold tap, its traditional source in Egypt.

At this point my wife, letting out the little yelp of the disoriented, dashed into the bedroom with a towel. The words printed on it were: 'SEMIRAMIS HOTEL.' Where the hell were we? And what were *our* names? Controlling my panic, I called the front desk and extracted a promise that someone would at least come to mend the loo. An hour and two phone calls later, a man did indeed arrive. He gave my wife, who answered the door, a bouquet *of dead flowers*, bowed and departed. We both agreed that this macabre piece of business showed a poetic flair that Buñuel, let alone Hitchcock, might have envied.

We turned in. The double bed, which looked innocuous enough, proved to have been resourcefully booby-trapped. Perhaps because its solitary occupant in the old Mameluke days had been an obese eunuch, it sloped so precipitously towards the middle that one had to hang on to the edge of the mattress with both hands to avoid rolling on to one's partner like a runaway boulder. My wife now asked me to turn off the lights. (I have mentioned that the room was set about with standard lamps). Since they did not respond to any of the wall-switches by the bed, I hauled myself out to deal with them

separately. Now came the touch of sheer genius. *None of them could be switched off.* We have all heard (or had experience) of hotel lights that will not turn *on*. But here was something far more baleful – a permanent blaze, as if at any moment the interrogation were about to begin. It finally became necessary in two cases to remove the plugs from their wall-sockets, in one to unscrew three red-hot bulbs, and in one to actually wrench the wire out of the wainscoting.

That was undoubtedly the Omar Khayyam's masterstroke, although throughout the next day small events took place that kept us on our toes. In response to an order of coffee for two, room service sent us two coffee-cups with a dwarf pot that held slightly less than enough for one. My pleas for a hot bath were answered by a waiter who escorted me 500 yards across the windswept grounds in my dressing-gown to a bungalow-type chalet containing a shower with a trickle of lukewarm water and no soap. When I asked for soap, he vanished altogether. Half an hour passed before I found out that he had delivered the soap to the chalet next door, apparently failing to observe that I was not in it.

As my wife and I lowered ourselves into bed for our second and last night, she pointed out a stump of wire protruding from the ceiling just over our heads, and wondered what it might be, or have been. All I could guess was that on some previous occasion a guest had so far failed to respond to the Khayyam treatment that he had actually *enjoyed* his exposure to the horrors of bourgeois life and showed no disposition to leave. 'Very well,' I pictured the Gyppu man saying on the fourth day. 'The time has come for stern measures. *Loosen the chandelier in Room 6 . . .*'

April 1972

'Waiter, there's a fly in my soup.'

'OK. Dig in!'

Clement Freud

MIXED ECONOMY

Sod the Value

'What's the grub like in your place?'

The difference between food and really sensational food is now so great that you would have every right to believe that they were prepared by different species of humanity.

I had 'good food' in Leicester last week. A friend who lives in those parts said, 'All right then, master; what's it to be: a caff with good grub or a restaurant with pretensions, chef in white hat and linen napkins?'

I flashed my Liberal Party membership card – and we went to the caff.

There was nothing wrong with the two whiskies which we drank at the bar. Prawn cocktails were fine; steak was huge, well hung sirloin, very rare (as we had ordered it) and they had had the good sense to put it in a low oven for a while before fiercely grilling it for a minute on each side so that the meat was beautifully undercooked and hot.

Chips were made from real potatoes, not very well made but, nevertheless, not powdered and called back to chip-shape; with St Ivel Stilton (why, oh why, did the company not stick to cream cheese which they do so well?) there was a Cox's apple peeled and sliced. We drank coffee; we had a bottle of 1981 Beaujolais, of which I have had many worse examples, and when the bill came I got change from a £20 note. Whiskies, wine, coffees, superb 12 oz sirloin, prawns, cheese, VAT ... and so we had another drink and wondered why it was that people went to prissy, pretentious, *nouvelle cuisine* phoneytoria and spent four times that. We had another drink and luxuriated in our well-being, brought on by a mixture of contentedness and value.

When the bill is less than you expect, the computer in your brain retrospectively reclassifies criticism. 'What a sensational menu,' I said on the way home, when I actually meant, 'What an amazingly low bill, considering.'

On the next day, an American friend came to London, told me that money was no object when it came to the pursuit of gastro-excellence and as he understood that there was a new three-star restaurant in town, had we not better go?

I suggested we go to the caff in Leicester; he said, 'Why?' I said, 'Terrific value,' and he said, 'Sod value, set your sights high.' So we went to Tante Claire, in the Royal Hospital Road, London. For a first course I had goose liver: just a plump, pink, whole, young goose liver; macerated, I should think for a day or two, in dry Madeira, then gently sizzled in clarified butter and placed atop a thin julienne of potatoes shaped like a beer-mat, then roasted and caramelised, all astride (*nouvelle cuisine* has sauce under the food) a light, translucent sauce in which there was a taste of raspberry vinegar; surrounding the liver were four small shallots, perfectly cooked so that they were brown on the outside and handsomely crisp in the middle.

The main course was a pig's trotter, boned (which is as delicate a job as knitting a vest of stinging nettles for a swan), stuffed with sweetbreads and cooked to a rigid, shining pinkness with small mounds of creamed baby turnips and a few straight French beans.

And for pudding, we had the best dessert I have eaten: an ice-cream flavoured with Armagnac, garnished with stoned alcoholic prunes; my friend also ate a selection of water ices made from run-of-the-mill material such as Kiwi fruit and persimmon.

When the bill came, he took it and I said, 'How much?' and he replied, 'Whatever it is, we had a great meal'; although he is only American, he was right.

Every now and then, you do come across dishes of such perfection, occasionally even whole meals of such undiluted excellence, that it would be worthwhile equating the high asking price of dinner for two *not* to the cost of six mediocre meals but to three days' fast and the joy of the memory.

Then might the world become a healthier, better place; poor restaurants would close through lack of those customers who stayed at home between smacking their lips in respect of last Tuesday's sea-bass in champagne morel sauce and salivating in expectation of next Monday's wild strawberry cake with apricot brandy – and getting thinner all the time.

If you were to ask what is the single factor that makes an outstanding cuisine, the answer is purchasing. Of course, the chef must be a man of genius, but, above all, the ingredients have to be perfect.

A mousseline sauce made with battery chicken egg yolks, any old butter from the supermarket shelf and a squeeze from the plastic lemon enriched with single cream can be cooked with all the skill of an Escoffier –

and not hold a candle to one cobbled together by a rent-a-cook using free-range eggs, dairy butter, freshly squeezed lemon and best double cream.

When you have made such a sauce, do not drape it over a frozen fillet of anonymous fish. Reserve it for a perfect artichoke, or a young fresh leek if times are hard.

The fact is that there is super food and acceptable food and restaurateurs try too hard to make you forget the fact by tarting up convenience packs to confuse you. I do not decry corned beef hash. It is a great dish for a trencherman and if you make it by mixing the contents of the tin from Argentina with the right amount of boiled, peeled, sliced new potatoes, onions simmered in butter, Dijon mustard, rock salt and coarsely ground white pepper all judged to a nicety, it has some pretensions to a place on a decent menu, but in the final analysis, the beef in the tin is old cow meat and it is a pity about all the good ingredients you deployed to disguise the fact.

May 1983

F. J. Cox

THE LIGHTNING LUNCHER

(A Wither-ing Retort)

[The *Lancet* condemns the proposal in favour of inaugurating a system of quick lunches for busy City men, and stigmatises it as 'a wicked physiological step.']

SHALL I, wasting precious hours
Over lunch, exhaust my powers
Dissipate my vital forces

Over dilatory courses,
Munch my lunch at ease and leisure,
Just to suit the *Lancet*'s pleasure?
  Howe'er quick the luncheon be,
  'Twill not be too quick for me!

City pace is far too fleet
To afford us time to eat;
So we pile up £ s. d.,
Bother physiology!
Though dyspeptic horrors follow,
Summary shall be each swallow –
  Howe'er quick the luncheon be,
  'Twill not be too quick for me!

Shall I, dallying o'er a steak,
Miss the deals that I might make?
Give, while golden moments range,
Time to chops instead of 'Change?
'Cause the *Lancet* cries, 'Go slow!'
Shall I cease to hurry? *No!*
  Howe'er quick the luncheon be,
  'Twill not be too quick for me!

'Time is money, money's time,'
There's the burden of my rhyme;
Clearly, then, the City needs
Automatic Ganymedes!
Could we find her, prized would she be,
Boon of boons – a clockwork Hebe!
  Howe'er quick her works might be,
  They'd not be too quick for me!

February 1903

Fay Maschler

MUSHROOMS

Alice was in Tesco's. She knew that she had come in for something but she couldn't remember what it was. Supermarkets seemed to keep changing. She could swear this one had changed once or twice since morning. 'What do you want?' asked a sulky-looking assistant. 'If I knew I would have asked you,' replied Alice crossly, and then fearing that she had offended his feelings, she said, 'I think when I came in I wanted some mushrooms.' 'If you wanted mushrooms when you came in, you'll want them when you go out!' said the assistant who looked uncommonly like a beetle and he turned his back. 'Oh dear,' thought Alice, now I *have* upset him and she went to look at the bottles of washing-up liquid. 'USE ME' one of them said and so Alice put it in her trolley.

The assistant came back. 'I have something important to say.' This sounded promising: Alice looked up at him. 'The mushrooms are in the cartons.' 'Is that your idea of being an assistant?' said Alice. 'It would make more sense it seems to me if you were called a shop deterrent.' But as she had

nothing else to do she thought she would go and look. The beetle, for she had decided that that is what he was, was right. The mushrooms were in a blue square plastic carton sealed over with plastic film. Each mushroom was almost completely round and extraordinarily white. Alice was beginning to feel crosser than ever. 'Mushrooms weren't like this yesterday,' she told herself. 'One mushroom will taste of another mushroom and neither of them will taste of anything,' said the beetle, but when Alice looked round he had scuttled out of sight.

'I may as well take them home,' she decided, 'because I know I was supposed to buy something and mushrooms used to be good on toast.'

When Alice got home she managed to prise the plastic film off the carton and discovered that the mushrooms were as smooth as marbles, though round the stem were specks of dirt that did not seem dirty. 'Soon I will find that water isn't wet!' said Alice peevishly

'I was really looking for somewhere a little more up-market in which to kill half-an-hour.'

and she called upstairs to her sister who was reading in the bedroom. 'Where have you been?' said Alice's sister, who was the one who had sent her out for the mushrooms. 'I had only begun this book when you left and now it is nearly finished.' 'Perhaps then you would be interested in some lunch,' said Alice snippily, but because she was a considerate, well brought-up girl really, she asked her sister how she would like them cooked.

Alice knew that most food had to be cooked so she was very surprised when her sister said that she would like the mushrooms in a salad. She took a sharp knife and holding it carefully (for she believed that a sharp knife would cut anyone who was careless *quite* badly) she cut the little buttons into neat slices. 'What pretty shapes!' thought Alice. 'They look like the border to the Persian carpet in our Mother's sitting room.'

Alice's sister crushed some garlic into olive oil before mixing in hardly any wine vinegar and some sea salt and black pepper and poured it over the mushroom slices that Alice had tipped into a bowl. 'We had better leave these for a while,' she said. 'I want to finish my chapter, so you must think of something else to do with the rest of the mushrooms.' And she went back upstairs.

Alice by now was exceedingly huffy and she picked up a mushroom and nibbled on one side. Nothing happened. She nibbled on the other side and nothing else happened. At that moment her cat Dinah came into the kitchen. 'Why don't you make mushroom ketchup?' said the cat. Alice didn't stop to think that this was the first time Dinah had talked to her, although she had in the past thought that Dinah had understood when she had to explain that there could be no saucer of milk because someone had clumsily upset it. She nibbled some more mushroom. 'Do cats like ketchup? Can you catch up with cats?' Alice was becoming confused. 'Dinah, my dear, do you have a recipe, because, although I know a great many things I don't think I know how to make ketchup?'

Dinah, it turned out, had been reading a copy of Jane Grigson's *The Mushroom Feast*, a fact which surprised Alice even more since she didn't know that cats could read or if

'As a matter of fact, this is my first time at a literary luncheon.'

PONT

THIS IS MR. CLOTHESBRUSH—

AND MISS THOMSON—

AND PROFESSOR CHURCHUR, WHO
INVENTED THE CHURCHUR—

AND CAPTAIN ELEPHANT
BIGTODAY—

AND MISS VINCENT—

AND MISS CARTER—

AND LADY HEIGH-HO—

AND MY BROTHER—

AND SIR WILLIAM GLOBBGLOB,
THE FAMOUS GLOSHSUSH—

AND MY OTHER BROTHER—

AND MISS THOMSON—

AND MISS TURNEDOUTATSLOU
EXPECT YOU SAW HER IN 'SE
NINES ARE EIGHTY-FOUR')—

AND THE DEAN OF WHYNOT-
ARRESTHER—

AND OF COURSE MY MOTHER—

AND MR. PASSDOWNTHECAR-
PLEASE, WHOM YOU MET LAST
TIME—

AND NOW I'M *sure* YOU WOU
LIKE SOMETHING TO DRINK

they could that they would choose to study recipe books. 'How queer everything is today,' she thought, 'but maybe it is because mushrooms no longer grow in fields but in cement sheds upon sterilized compost.'

Dinah asked if she were ready to hear the recipe. This is what she said: 'Take 3 lbs mushrooms, 3 ounces salt, $\frac{1}{2}$ pint wine vinegar, 2 teaspoons chopped onion, 1 level teaspoon peppercorns, 1 level teaspoon all-spice, 2 blades of mace, $\frac{1}{2}$ teaspoon whole cloves and a $\frac{1}{2}$-inch piece of cinnamon. Chop the mushrooms, spread them out in a large bowl and sprinkle the salt over them. Leave them, covered, for two days, stirring and squashing them occasionally. Put with the remaining ingredients into a large pan and simmer for about two hours. Leave the lid off and the liquor will concentrate to a good strong flavour. Pour through a cloth into hot sterilised bottles and seal immediately. If you are using thin-necked sauce bottles, strain the liquor into a clean pan, bring back to the boil and pour into the bottles through a muslin lined funnel.'

'That sounds very nice, Dinah dear. Is it as nice as mice?' And, Alice added petulantly, 'What do you use it for?'

Dinah said that it was useful for flavouring many dishes and might easily perk up a sauce. 'Well, I must go now,' said Dinah. 'I haven't finished last Sunday's papers.' 'Curiouser and curiouser,' thought Alice and turned to the rest of the mushrooms.

Suddenly there was a loud sniff in the corner of the kitchen and Alice could just make out a figure chopping up shallots. It seemed from the way she was dressed that she was a Duchess. 'What are you doing?' she asked fractiously. 'Doing as I would be done by, you silly child,' replied the Duchess, 'making *duwelles*.'

'You are using far too many shallots,' said Alice, but the Duchess just sniffed. She cooked the shallots in butter and oil and added finely chopped mushrooms and

parsley and cooked stirring until the mixture was dry. Alice took them away from her and stored them in small pots in the freezer. She popped the remaining mushroom in her mouth but still she couldn't taste anything.

May 1980

Paul Theroux

ALGEBRA

Ronald had threatened to move out before, but I always begged him not to. He knew he had power over me. He was one of those people who treats flattery as if it is mockery, and regards insult as a form of endearment. You couldn't talk to him. He refused to be praised, and if I called him 'Fanny' he only laughed. I suppose he knew that basically he was worthless, which led him to a kind of desperate boasting about his faults – he even boasted about his impotence. What Ronnie liked best was to get drunk on the cheap wine he called 'Parafino' and sprawl on the chaise and dig little hornets out of his nose and say what scum most people were. I knew he was bad for me and that I would have another breakdown if things went on like this much longer.

'God's been awful good to me,' he said once in the American accent he affected when he was drunk.

'That's blasphemy,' I said. 'You don't mean that. You'll go to Hell.'

'Wrong!' he shrieked. 'If you *do* mean it you'll go to Hell.'

When I met him he had just joined How-letts, the publisher. Quite early on, he began to sneer at the parties he sometimes took me to by boasting that he could go to one every day of the week. I thought he had a responsible position but afterwards, when I got to know the others, particularly Phillipa and Roger, I came to realize that he was a rather insignificant person in the firm. I think this is why he seemed so embarrassed to have me along and took me so seldom. He implied that I wasn't attractive or intelligent enough for his publishing friends, and he would not let me near the real writers.

'This is Michael Insole, a friend,' he'd say, never letting on that we were living together in my flat. That sort of thing left me feeling incredibly depressed.

Then everything changed. I have not really analysed it until now. It certainly wasn't an idea – nothing as solemn or calculated as that. It was more an impulse, a frenzy you might say, or a leap in the dark. At one of the parties I was talking to Sir Charles Moonman, the novelist and critic. 'And what do you do?' he asked me. At another time I might have said, 'I live with Ronald Brill,' but I was feeling so fed up with Ronnie I said, 'Basically, I'm a writer.'

'Do I know your work?' asked Sir Charles.

'No,' I said. It was the truth. I worked then, as I do now, at the Arcade Off-Licence near the Clapham South tube station, but living with Ronnie had made me want to go into writing.

Sir Charles found my prompt reply very funny, and then an odd thing happened. He relaxed and began to talk and talk. He was hugely old and had the downright manner and good health of a country doctor. He was reading Kingsley, he said, and squeezed air with his hands. He described the book, but it was nothing like any Kingsley I had ever read. He said, 'It has, don't you agree, just the right tone, an elasticity one associates with fiction –' I nodded and tried to add something of my own, but could not get a word in.

At this point, Virginia Byward, the novel-ist and traveller, ambled over and said hello.

'This is Mister Insole. He's a writer,' said Sir Charles. 'We've just been talking about Kinglake.'

Kinglake, not Kingsley. I was glad I had not said anything.

'*Eothen*? That Kinglake?' said Miss Byward.

'*The Invasion of the Crimea*. That Kinglake,' said Sir Charles.

'Well, I'll let you two get on with it,' said Miss Byward, laughing at her mistake. 'Very nice to have met you, Mister Insole.'

'She's so sweet,' said Sir Charles. 'And her reportage is devastating.' He clawed at his cuff. 'Bother. It's gone eight. I must rush – dinner engagement.'

'I'll be late for mine, as well,' I said. 'My hostess will tear a strip off me.' But I was not going anywhere.

'Such a bore, isn't it?' he said. 'We are both being called away. So unfortunate. I would much rather stand and chat about the Crimean War.'

'So would I!' I said. Then, I could think of nothing else to say, so I said, 'I am one of your most passionate fans.'

This was my leap in the dark. I had never read a word he had written. I suppose I looked terrified, but you would not have known it from the look on Sir Charles's face – pure joy. He removed his pipe from his mouth and stuffed his finger in the bowl.

'I'm so glad.'

'I'm not joking,' I said. 'I find your work a real consolation. It genuinely engages me.'

'It is awfully good of you to say so.'

He sounded as if he meant it. More than that, he reacted as if no-one had ever said these words to him before.

'We must meet for lunch one day.' He clenched the pipestem in his teeth and beamed.

I said, 'How about dinner at my place? When you're free.'

And Sir Charles Moonman, the eminent

novelist and critic, said to me, 'I am free most evenings.'

'Next week?'

'I can do Monday, or Tuesday, or – '

'Monday,' I said. I gave him my address and that was that. He clapped me on the shoulder in his bluff country doctor way, and I was still somewhat dazed when Ronald came over.

'What are you grinning about?'

'I've just invited Sir Charles Moonman for dinner.'

Ronald was horrified. 'You can't,' he said. 'I'll phone him in the morning and tell him it's off.'

'You'll do no such thing,' I said, raising my voice to a pitch that had Ronald shushing me and steering me to a corner.

'What are you going to give him?'

He had me there. I do a nice shepherd's pie, and Ronald has often praised my flan, but truly I had not given the menu much thought, and told him so.

'Shepherd's pie!' Ronald was saying as Virginia Byward sidled up to me.

'Hello, Mr Insole,' she said. She had remembered my name! 'Has Charles gone?'

Ronald was speechless.

'Charles had to be off,' I said. 'A dinner party – he was rather dreading it.'

Miss Byward was staring at Ronald.

'I know Mr Insole is a writer,' she said. 'But what do you do?'

Ronald turned purple. He said, 'I sell worthless books,' and marched away.

'I hope I didn't say anything to offend him,' said Miss Byward. 'Too bad about Charles. I was hoping he'd still be here. I meant to lock horns with him.'

'If you're free on Monday, come along for dinner. Charles will be there.'

'I couldn't crash your dinner party.'

'Be my guest,' I said. 'It won't be fancy, but I think of myself as a good plain cook.'

'If you're sure it's no trouble –'

'I'd be honoured,' I said, and then I could think of nothing to say except, 'I am one of your most passionate fans,' the statement that had gone down so well with Sir Charles. I was a bit embarrassed about saying it, because repeating it made it sound formulated and insincere. But it was my embarrassment that brought it off.

'Are you?' she said. She was clearly delighted.

'Your reportage is devastating.'

It was as easy as twisting a tap. I said nothing more. I simply listened to her talk, and finally she said, 'I've so enjoyed our little chat. See you Monday.'

Ronald was silent on the way home until we got to Kennington or The Oval. Then he said, 'Are you a writer?'

At Stockwell, I said. 'Are you a publisher?'

As the train drew into Clapham Common, he stood up and said, 'You're shameless.' He pushed past me and ran up the escalator.

That night Ronald slept on the chaise and the next day he moved out of the flat and out of my life.

I had not known how easy it would be to make the acquaintance of Sir Charles Moonman and Miss Byward. It had only been necessary to learn a new language, and it was one that Ronald either despised or did not know. When I went broody about Ronald's absence over the weekend I remembered the guests I'd invited for Monday and I cheered up.

But on Sunday I began to worry about the numbers. Three people did not seem much of a dinner party and I kept hearing myself saying, 'I like the intimate sort of party.' So I invited Mr Momma, too. Mr Momma, a Cypriot, was a housepainter who lived in the top floor flat. He never washed his milk bottles, so Ronald had named him 'Inky', which was short for 'inconsiderate'. Mr Momma said he would do a salad.

On the Monday I went to the library and got copies of Sir Charles's and Miss

Byward's books. I was setting them out, arranging them on tables, when the phone went. I must have been feeling a bit insecure still because I thought at once that it was either Sir Charles or Miss Byward who had rung to say they couldn't make it after all.

'Michael?'

It was Tanya Moult, one of Ronald's authors. I should say one of Ronald's victims, because he had strung her along for years. She was working on a book about pirates, women pirates, and Ronald had said it was just the ticket, a kind of robust woman's thing. That was very Ronald. He had other people doing books on cowboys – black cowboys; hairdressers and cooks – all men; gay heroes, and cats in history. Tanya sent him chapters and at the same time she scraped a living writing stories for women's magazines under a pseudonym. Ronald was very possessive about Tanya, but perversely so: he kept me away from her while at the same time being nasty to her.

I told her that Ronald had moved out. It was the first she had heard of it and I could tell that she was really down. Ronald had not been in touch with her about her newest chapter.

'Look, Tanya,' I said – it was the first time I had used her Christian name. 'Why don't you come round tonight? I'm having a few friends over for dinner.'

She hesitated. I knew what she was thinking - I couldn't blame her.

'Sir Charles Moonman,' I said. 'And Virginia Byward.'

'Gosh, Michael, really?'

'And Mr Momma from upstairs.'

'I've met him,' she said. 'I don't know whether I have anything to wear.'

'Strictly informal. If I know Sir Charles he'll be wearing an old cardigan, and Virginia will be in a rather shapeless tunic.'

She said she would be there. At seven, Mr Momma appeared in a bulging blue jumpsuit, carrying plastic bags of lettuce and onions and some tubs of dressing. He said. 'How do you know I like parties?' and pulled one bulge out of his pocket – an avocado. His teeth were big, one was cracked, he wore a gold crucifix on a chain around his neck, and he smelled of sweat and soap. He sniffed. 'Cooking food!' He swung his bags on to the table. 'Salad,' he said. 'I make fresh. Like my madder.'

I had never seen Mr Momma happier. He shooed me out of the kitchen and then busied himself chopping and grating, and whistling through the crack in his tooth.

Tanya arrived on the dot of eight with a bottle of Hungarian Riesling. 'I'm so excited,' she said, and I realised just how calm I was. Then the bell rang again.

'Oh, my God,' cried Mr Momma.

Tanya went to the kitchen door and smiled.

'Like my madder,' Mr Momma said.

Sir Charles was breathless when I met him on the landing.

'I should have warned you about those stairs,' I said.

But his breathlessness helped. He was panting, as if he had been cornered after a long chase and he could do nothing but smile and gasp his thanks as he was introduced to Tanya. He found a chair and propelled himself backwards into it and sighed.

'Wine?' I said.

'That would be lovely.'

I poured him a glass of Montrachet, gave him its pedigree (but omitted that fact that I had got it at a staff discount from Arcade Off-Licence) and left him to Tanya.

'– it's not generally known, but there were a fantastic number,' Tanya was saying, and she was off: women pirates. Sir Charles was captivated.

'Do you know,' said Virginia Byward when she arrived, glancing around the flat and relaxing at the sight of two copies of her books, 'this is only the second time in my life I've been to Clapham? I'd rather not talk about the first time. I came a cropper that night!' She spoke to Sir Charles. 'It was during the war.'

'Something for your biographer,' said Sir Charles.

We all laughed at this. But I thought then, and I continued to think throughout the evening, that I was now a part of their lives and that the time they were spending with me mattered. Each great writer seems to me to contain a posthumous book, the necessary and certain biography. Writers carry this assurance of posterity around with them. This was a page of that book.

This: my chaise, on which Miss Byward was sitting; my brass Benares ashtray with a smoldering thimble-shape of Sir Charles's pipe tobacco in it; my tumbling Tradescantia; my gate-legged dining table on which one of Ronald's dents was still visible; my footstool with its brocade cushion; my crystal sugar bowl; the wine glass Miss Byward was holding, the pillow Tanya was hugging; my basketwork fruit holder; me.

I excused myself and went into the kitchen. Mr Momma was putting the finishing touches to his salad. He had made a little hill of chopped lettuce leaves and sprinkled it with olives and pimentoes and drips of dressing.

'You love it?'

I said it was perfect.

'It is a woman's tee-tee,' he said, and made a knob-turning gesture with his hand.

In the parlour, my other guests were engrossed in conversation. I thought they were talking about an author they all respected; a name seemed to repeat (*Murray? Gilbert Murray?*). I pretended to straighten the leg of the table so I could get the drift of their conversation, but I quickly grasped that they were talking about money. (And I heard myself saying on a future occasion, *I thought they were talking about an author they all respected . . .*)

'I don't know how some people manage,' said Sir Charles. 'I really don't. By the way, Michael, this wine is superb. You didn't tell me you had a cellar.'

'I have an attic too,' I said.

'Isn't he a poppet!' said Virginia.

Mr Momma brought out his salad.

'Bravo,' said Virginia, and hearing Mr Momma's accent, she asked him where he was from. His mention of Cyprus had Virginia asking him which particular village was his and brought a long very practised-sounding story from Sir Charles about a hotel in Limassol. Throughout the meal we talked intimately about Lawrence Durrell and I even found myself chipping in every now and then. I could see that it was considered quite a coup to have Mr Momma on hand.

'And what is our friend from Cyprus doing in London?' asked Virginia.

'I am a painter.'

Mr Momma did not have the English to amplify this. He was quickly taken to be a tormented artist in exile rather than the hardworking house painter he was. We talked about the Mediterranean sense of colour, and afterwards Mr Momma ran upstairs for his Cypriot records. He played them, he danced with Virginia, and he told her he loved her. Then he sat down and sobbed into his handkerchief.

'I've been admiring this wine glass,' said Virginia over Mr Momma's muted hoots. 'Is it part of a set?'

I said, 'Just the one,' and filled it with the claret I had brought out for the shepherd's pie.

I was relieved when Sir Charles said he had to go, because that was my signal to open the Krug, which went down a treat. Then Sir Charles and Virginia shared a taxi back to Hampstead and Tanya (making a crack about Ronald) said she had never enjoyed herself more. Hearing what Tanya had said, Mr Momma put his arm around me. He smelled strenuously of his dancing.

'No,' I said, and led him to the door. 'Let's not spoil it.'

I slept alone, but I was not alone. The evening had been a great success. Both Sir Charles and Virginia sent me notes, thanking me for having them. They were brief notes, but I replied saying that the pleasure had been all mine.

Afterwards, I wondered why they had agreed to come. I decided that their very position had something to do with it. They were so grand that most people thought that they must be very busy, so no one dared to invite them. And people believed that they were beyond praise. But my flattery, my offer of a meal, my discount wines had done the trick.

I had worked hard to make the evening festive, and Mr Momma had been an unexpected success. And what had I asked of them? Nothing – nothing but for them to be there.

I had told them I was a writer. Because I had said this no one talked about it: I was one of them. Anyway, a good host is preoccupied with managing his party. His graciousness is silence when it is not encouragement. He isn't supposed to say much, only to keep the dishes coming and the glasses filled. So, in the end, they did not know much about me. They talked to each other.

The proof that Miss Byward meant what she said about enjoying herself was her invitation to me several weeks later for drinks at her very tiny flat in Hampstead. It was not until I saw her flat that I fully understood how she could have seen something to admire in mine. She was clearly an untidy person, but I was grateful when she introduced me as 'Michael Insole, the writer'. There were six others there, all writers whose names I instantly recognized, but because of the seating arrangements, I had no choice but to talk to Wibbert the poet. He told me a very entertaining story about giving a poetry reading in Birmingham, and he finished by saying, 'The pay's appalling.

They always apologise when they hand it over.'

Henry Wibbert was a tall balding youth with the trace of a regional accent, and bitten fingernails, something I had always hated until I met him. His socks had slipped into his shoes and I could see his white ankles. His poet's love of failure was written all over him, and when I told him I did not write poetry he seemed to take this as a criticism – as if I was acting superior – and I wanted to tell him that, in fact, I had never written anything at all.

'I do the odd spot of reviewing,' he said, somewhat defensively. And then, 'I can always go back to teaching yobboes if I find myself really hard up.' He twisted his finger into his mouth and chewed. 'I'm sure your earnings have you in the super-tax bracket.'

'Far from it,' I said. 'I find it very hard to manage.'

At once, he was friendlier, we had found common ground as struggling writers.

'It's hand to mouth with me,' he said.

I said, 'I was having this very conversation with Sir Charles Moonman just the other night.'

'He hasn't got my worries,' said Wibbert, though when I had said Sir Charles's name Wibbert looked closely at me, the way a person peers from a high window to an interesting spectacle below.

'You'd be surprised.'

'If it was a struggle for that pompous overpraised old bastard?' he said. 'Yes, I'd be very surprised.'

'Have you ever met him?'

Wibbert shook his head.

'Why don't you come over some evening? You might change your mind.'

Wibbert said, 'He'd probably hate me.'

'Absolutely not,' I said.

'How can you be so sure?'

'Because I'm sure he's read your poetry, and if he has how could he fail to be an admirer of yours?'

This did the trick. Wibbert wrote his telephone number on the back of my hand in ballpoint, and as he had to hold my hand in his in order to do this it was noticed by others at Miss Byward's as a rather eloquent gesture.

'You're not leaving,' said Miss Byward, when I asked for my cape.

'A dinner engagement. Unfortunately. I would so much rather stay here and chat. It's been lovely.'

She released me and afterwards I wondered whether she had not said those very words to me. On the bus home I thought how much more satisfying it was to be a host than a guest.

I went home and after four tries typed a letter to Sir Charles, which I copied out in long-hand – I liked the look of spontaneous intimacy in a handwritten letter. I was sure he would appreciate it. I told him about Wibbert and said that Wibbert was dead keen to meet him, if we could fix a day.

The reply from Sir Charles came in the form of an invitation from the Royal Society of Literature in which I was named as his guest at a lecture by Cyril Crowder on 'Our Debt to Hugh Walpole.' Although a reply was not requested I dashed off a note to the Society's secretary and said I'd be delighted to attend. And another to Sir Charles. On the day, I was so impatient I arrived early and chatted to the only person I could find, a little old lady fussing at a table. I had very nearly invited her to meet Sir Charles when she revealed herself as one of the tea ladies and said, 'I should have a cream bun now if I was you. They're always the first to go.'

Just before the lecture the room filled with people, Sir Charles among them. I blushed when a man, on being introduced to me by Sir Charles, said yes, indeed, he knew my work well. Sir Charles was pleased, and so was I, but I quickly took myself to a corner of the room. Here, a group of people were talking to a man who was obviously the centre of attraction. I made a bee-line for this man, but instead of speaking, simply listened to what the others were saying. The man smiled at me a number of times.

'His friendship with James amounted to influence,' someone said. 'I believe it was very great.'

'Deep,' said the man, and smiled at me. I swallowed my fear and said. 'Profound.'

'That's it,' said the man and thanked me with his eyes.

'They're calling you, Cyril,' said a woman. 'You're on.'

This was Cyril Crowder! But he took his time. He said, 'You'll have to excuse me. I must do my stuff. Perhaps I'll see you afterwards. There are drinks downstairs in the Lodge.'

Cyprus sherry, Hungarian Bulls Blood that was red ink, a semi-sweet Spanish white and a mongrel Corsican rosé.

The dinner I gave for Cyril Crowder, Sir Charles and Lady Barbara, Virginia Byward and Wibbert, was one of my most memorable. I was further enhanced by the appearance after dinner (I had only six chairs) of Tanya and Mr Momma – and Mr Momma brought his records. Naturally I left them to themselves, kept their glasses filled with some vintage Muscadet (1971) and let them become quite tipsy. Very late in the evening, Cyril took me aside. I told him again how much I had enjoyed his lecture, but he interrupted, saying, 'Have you ever thought of addressing the Society?'

'I wouldn't dare.'

'Oh, do.'

'I'm not even a member,' I said.

'We can put that right,' he said, and he hollered across the room, 'Charles – how about making Michael a Fellow at the next committee meeting? All in favour say, "Aye"!'

'Aye!' came the shout from the sofa.

And Mr Momma said, 'High!'

'Motion carried,' said Cyril. 'Now what will you speak on?'

'First things first,' I said, and uncorked a bottle of port (1972), decanted it through my hanky and poured three inches into a schooner.

'That wine's a gentleman,' said Cyril.

'So you can understand why I was so keen to lay it down.'

After Sir Charles and Lady Barbara left, Mr Momma put his records on the gramophone and did his drunken Cypriot shuffle. Wibbert waltzed with Tanya. I was tapped on the shoulder. Cyril had taken off his spectacles. He said, 'May I have the pleasure?' and slipped his arm around my waist.

Friendship is algebra, but there are operations most people are too impatient or selfish to perform. Any number is possible! There is a cynical side to this. Ronald used to say that you can sleep with anyone you like – you only have to ask. That is almost entirely selfish. But one can be unselfish, even in sleeping around – in giving everything and expecting nothing but agreeable

A SUNDAY DINNER.

Father of Family (who has accidentally shot the leg of a Fowl under the table). 'MIND T'DOG DOESN'T GET IT!'
Young Hopeful (triumphantly). 'ALL RIGHT, FEYTHER! I'VE GOTTEN ME FOOT ON IT!'

company. 'Giving everything,' I say; but so little is actually required – a good natured remark, a little flattery, a drink.

But I have been bold. Not long after my election to the Royal Society I saw a production of *A Streetcar Named Desire*, with Annette Frame playing Blanche Dubois. I wrote her a fan letter. She replied. I replied. We exchanged letters on a weekly basis – mine were letters, hers postcards. Then I popped the question. Would she join me for a drink? We agreed on a date and though she was leery at first she stayed until the wee hours. Now I count her as one of my dearest friends. Algebra.

I sometimes think that in my modest way I have discovered something that no-one else knows. When Virginia Byward got her O.B.E. it was I who helped her choose her dress and I who drove her to the Palace. A year before I would not have believed it to be possible, and yet as we rounded Hyde Park Corner I realised we were hurrying to meet the Queen. 'Alice,' Virginia calls me when she is a little tipsy and tearful. But the life I have is the life I have always wanted. I am surprised that no-one has realised how simple it is.

Once, I thought that in agreeing to attend my parties these people were doing me an enormous favour, taking time off from busy schedules to flatter my vanity. Later I saw how empty their lives were. 'I'd have lunch with anyone remotely human,' Wibbert once said. It was the saddest thing I had ever heard. Now it is clear that if it were not for me they would drearily write their books and live drearily alone and be too proud and unimaginative to invite each other round.

They take me as I am. I pose no threat; but more, I believe I have brought some joy into their lives – as much into Mr Momma's as Sir Charles's. It is only awkward when, very late in the evening, their gratitude gets the better of them and they insist on hearing something about my latest book. I say it's dreadful, everything's up the wall, I haven't written a word for ages. And they accept this. They even seem a bit relieved when I change the subject and uncork another bottle.

March 1979

Susan Jeffreys

FAMILY PACK

'My grandfather considered any room under 8,000 calories to be unfurnished.'

'Why don't you buy a dog? You're a dog cook. Honest. You think you're cooking for a load of dogs.'

How we loved to quote from the classics during family meals. That line of Pinter's was repeated as often as my grandmother's macaroni cheese. Not that all her cooking was lousy; in fact, her roast dinners were very fine indeed, but when she strayed away from meat and two veg, things went badly wrong. Her bread and butter puddings were like the Sargasso sea with becalmed hulks of bread half-submerged in a scummy sea of milk.

Mind you, there was little incentive to cook anything decent for us – we were far from couth. The chromosomes that carry essential information about table manners had never made it into the family's genetic pool. I come from a long line of messy troughers.

'Would you like a dessert?'

'Yes, I think I would. That bit over there by the sink looks rather good. I'll try a slice of that if I might.'

'How about some cheese to follow? I think

there's still a good chunk wedged under the fridge.'

You could eat off our kitchen floor. Very well, actually.

Generations of sloppy eaters have given a rich and sustaining patina to the floorboards in the family hovel. You can't get an effect like that just by slinging the gravy around – you have to be born to the craft. As for the unifying flecks of oatmeal and Bisto that link our walls and curtains, no interior designer could recreate them. It takes years, and breeding, to make a home look like that.

My grandfather liked to have food around him at all times: up the walls, on the carpet, tucked behind the furniture. He kept a supply of cold sausages in his sock drawer and a ration of chocolate and garlic stuffed down the sides of his armchair. He considered any room under 8,000 calories to be unfurnished.

At meal times he was dangerous as well as messy. The fork made it to the English table around 1460 but it never found favour with my grandfather; he was essentially a knife man. Food that couldn't be impaled was not worth eating in his book. He would load portions of grub on to a particularly long and fierce carving knife and lunge about the table with it. If you wanted to eat, you had to grapple with fork and plate for a helping. The diffident with short arms went to the wall.

My grandmother sat on his right side, not

because it was some ancient and courtly mark of rank but in order to get first crack at the good stuff. I never saw her in her prime – she was in her seventies when I messed with her, but I remember her as quick. Those who ate with her during the war years and rationing spoke with awe of her speed. They said she'd be on to her prey like a Messerschmitt – you only saw the flash of light on her knife and fork and by then it was too late.

Time passed, much gravy flowed under the table and in the fulness of time my grandparents handed in their dinner-pails. A wind of change blew through the kitchen and we decided to clean up our ingesting act. There'd be no more 'cooking for a load of dogs'; we were going to get ourselves some etiquette. We hired a skip for the old sausages and a sand-blaster for the gravy stains. Before long we were putting the custard in a jug and keeping a separate spoon for the condensed milk tin. We were on the long climb that leads to napkins and salad dishes.

In a new mood of fair shares for all we bought a serving-out spoon. There was to be no more grappling with fork and knife; instead, food was going to be passed around in dinky little dishes and put on to the plate via the new spoon. The meals of the long knife were over and we no longer had to keep the Elastoplast next to the pepper and salt.

Table manners were introduced. Shouting with your mouth full was out, so was jabbing with a loaded fork or pointing the bone. Elbows were to be kept off the table at all times and that same sweeping rule applied to feet. We were no longer the 'load of dogs' from Pinter's *Homecoming* – but we never quite made it to the napkins and salad plates. Something held us back from being couth.

Like the Kennedys, we knew that a family that ate together stayed together, but look what it did for them. We knew that family meals were a special time, perhaps the only moment when the whole family were gathered together. We never neglected this opportunity to go through the day's events, count the takings from the pool-tables and call each other a pack of bastard ingrates.

It was these meal-time conversations that held us back from gracious living, so we had a big drive on reading at table. Everyone was forced to take it up, with extra portions awarded to those reading an atlas or a large-format newspaper. Meals were timed to coincide with *The Archers* and dinner-time conversation came to an end. Nearly a decade of blissfully silent eating followed, broken only by the noise of a turning page or Clarrie Grundy in labour.

I smuggled a husband, and my brother several women, to the family table. Behind the wall of silence, they went unnoticed. The roast potatoes didn't go so far but the peace remained unbroken. It was not to last. Nature is cruel and before long we heard the clatter of little pushers; when we lowered our papers we found we needed an extra leaf in the table and a plastic cloth.

Things are far worse now than they were in my grandfather's days – even the ceiling's got gravy on it now. Our children eat with a savagery and abandon that appals even us. They do things with custard that would make your hair stand on end, keep a regular check on gravity with plates of stew, and have a hundred and one ways with a fish finger.

Worse still, the whole family are reduced to eating in their vests like Italian peasants in order to keep the top layer of clothing free from grease. It's a terrible sight to see us at table – worthy of *The Homecoming*.

We never made it to the napkins and salad plates, never even made it halfway to gentility. Dogs to dogs in three generations.

July 1985

E. V. Knox

OYSTERIA

THE oysters of Great Britain
   Were brought to JULIUS CAESAR;
He bolted them unbitten
   And smiled like *Mona Lisa.*

The Emperor AUGUSTUS
   Preferred them put in patties.
His cook, whose name was Justus
   Could never serve him satis.

The Emperor TIBERIUS,
   A man debased and selfish,
Was never wholly serious
   Except about these shellfish.

And CLAUDIUS and CALIGULA
   Made quite a ceremonium
Of eating this particular
   Subaqueous *obsonium.*

Why should I dwell on NERO,
   Who gave the earliest charters
To oystermen – the hero
   Of all save Christian martyrs?

I will not speak of OTHO,
   Nor GALBA the rebellious,
Nor tell the tales I know (though
   Superb) about VITELLIUS.

I will not say how TITUS
   Once murmured to VESPASIAN,
'Shall oysters not delight us
   On this unique occasion?'

Enough to point out clearly
   How Romans, blonde or dusky,
Admired and cherished dearly
   These delicate molluscae.

('They seem to suit my carcase,
   Hic cibus est divinus,'
Said HADRIAN; so did MARCUS
   AURELIUS ANTONINUS.

And once the great HONORIUS
   Broke down through sheer repletion,
Striving to burst the glorious
   Record of DIOCLETIAN.)

    ★   ★   ★

Rome fell. There came a silence;
   I cannot disentangle
How oysters in these islands
   Fared underneath the Angle.

Who knows how much the oyster
   Suffered amongst the rages
Of feudal keep and cloister
   That marred the Middle Ages?

I merely guess the Normans,
   To prove they were no caitiffs,
Put up a stout performance
   In dealing with our natives.

And oysters, nicely nourished
   And baffling all intruders,
Still held their own and flourished
   Right down into the TUDORS.

The TUDORS and their cousins
   With appetite and unction
Kept wolfing them by dozens
   At many a stately function.

And later kings who followed
   With tears of deep devotion
Ecstatically swallowed
   This tit-bit of the ocean;

Till the four early GEORGES
   Made it an act of schism
Not to indulge in orgies
   Of ostreophilism.

And still with each September,
 When oysters shine so pleasantly,
All loyal hearts remember
 To feed on them incessantly.

Much may have waned and faltered;
 The oyster, our palladium,
Abides with us unaltered
 And costs far less than radium.

The price? The price is hateful.
 But what is that to me, Sir?
Give me another plateful
 Like those you gave to CAESAR!

September 1929

Joan Bakewell

KITCHEN SHOPS

It's a case of nice wok if you can get it. No, *wok*; the instruction leaflet describes it as 'essential'. And you've never heard of it. It's people like you who think a Chinese steamer is something that once took lady missionaries up the Yangtse. Call yourself a cook!

To do just that these days, it's no good boasting of having learnt at mother's apron-strings a strong grounding in our national dishes: Yorkshire pudding in gravy for starters, cloves in the apple pie, cabinet pudding – that sort of thing. All that is taken for granted. To call yourself a cook within thumbing distance of *The Good Food Guide*, you need a thorough grounding in several cultures and the nicer points of international cuisine only easily acquired in the canteen of the United Nations.

You must know what the Japanese and the Welsh do with seaweed, and the Eskimos with pemmican, what a yabbie is to an Australian and an Om Ali to an Egyptian. It helps to have a smattering of six languages, the dexterity of a concert pianist, hands like asbestos and a sound knowledge of Thermal Dynamics. You will also need a wardrobe of oven gloves and a butcher's apron, a kitchen installed like a space station and furnished with the bric-a-brac of a peasant's cottage. You'll need dishes specially shaped for avocados, others for artichokes, prongs to hold sweetcorn, brochettes to spear kebabs, thermometers to measure things either coming to the boil or freezing solid for weeks. You'll need a larding needle for threading lard, a stoner for olives and cherries, a gingerbread cutter, roast baster and, of course, a wok. Thankfully, we have the kitchen shops to help us.

Something very odd is happening to our kitchens. Time was when labour-saving was all the rage. The nation's wives, chuffed with new jobs and even new careers, were only too pleased to pop a handful of things in the pressure-cooker and leave it at that. Frozen and tinned food got better in quality, more varied in range. Cook books dealt with how to mix and disguise already prepared foods. The commercials harked on about 'They'll never guess it wasn't your own home cooking.'

Then suddenly two-income homes found themselves with abundant money, friends to impress and enough leisure to indulge in a bit of high living. And so cooking got classy. The kitchen became the focal point of social display, its produce indicated your standing on the OK ladder, and the nature of gadgetry changed direction. It ceased being labour-saving and became deliberately time consuming. How else explain growing your own herbs, baking your own bread, brewing your own beer, making your own yoghourt. 'It only takes minutes, honestly ...' they say. Exactly. Minutes longer than not doing it.

And of course it all needs equipment. But at the same time as cooking got classy, it also reverted to the primitive. Marie Antoinette never had it so good. Nowadays housewives in Virginia Water with a Volvo in the garage and an account at Harrods are playing at being French peasants littering their kitchens with wooden spoons, cane baskets, crude pottery from Brittany and Portugal that costs pence over there but a fortune over here.

What's more, they make things hard for themselves, beating eggs with bound twigs, turning the handle on coffee beans till their elbows ache. And it's not just stockbroker wives. The obsession has a hold on the menfolk too. 'How long do you take making your curries, then?' 'Oh, several days.' 'Good man.' That was heard not at the checkout desk at Sainsbury's, evening cookery at the local Poly, the dinner table of old colonials. It was the smalltalk of editors at a powerhouse of BBC Current Affairs, not 100 miles from Robin Day's elbow. Ask them if you must know what a wok is.

But among all this knowingness, certain and subtle distinctions are to be observed. I have an unprovable theory that correct spell-

'BRING HER ANOTHER DUCK, WAITER.'

ing was invented by the Victorian upper classes when working people learnt to read. Just enough accuracy to set them apart. Thus with cooking: while baked beans and fish fingers are the fodder of hurried family life, those with leisure and money expend it on their new-found new-fangled domestic skills. So on the one side of the high street you find the good old hardware store dense with Pyrex dishes, tin openers, roasting trays and Thermos flasks. Across the street, at somewhere coyly calling itself Patsy's Pinnie or The Apple Fool, all is copper-bottomed, cast iron, baking bricks and barbecues.

I love them both. They are both Aladdin's Caves of goodies, their stock stacked to the ceiling, even dangling from it, and smelling of paraffin and furniture polish, or thyme and coffee beans. They are professional shops and we are all professionals seeking expertise in the execution of soufflés, the perfecting of pancakes, asking advice about frying pans. Good old hardware will go for Teflon; trendy nostalgia will insist on cast iron.

The shoppers are as intriguing as the goods: smock and sandals buying something that smokes their own fish: Mum plus pram and three buying wax cases for birthday jellies. We are finally all artisans in our own kitchens, concentrating with eager diligence on how to make and enjoy making what will nourish those we love. It is a worthy way to spend money. Perhaps Marie Antoinette was right after all. I wonder whether she had a good recipe for cake.

June 1980

'*It's so much more satisfying when one drives out into the country and gets one's own chutney.*'

Gwyn Thomas

GRACE AND GRAVY

I would, on balance, given a better eye and a stronger wrist, have preferred to be a wood-chopper rather than a teacher. At least the blocks and faggots do not walk around with your traumas notched in decorative designs all over them. Nor do they need school dinners.

In the second school at which I taught the eating scheme when I got there was strictly out of Gorki. The dining-hall was the school library, a small, gloomy room. The books themselves did not help. They fell into two main types. Books like *Old Saint Paul's* and *Last of the Barons* and *The Drunkard's Dream* donated by a school governor who was not much for reading himself but who was for other people's reading being wholesome. The other section of the library had been the personal property of a past master, an eccentric polymath who had not been able to resist any volume over five hundred pages. He had gone through life awaiting the revelation of something tremendous. In some lump of leather-bound wisdom he was convinced he would find it and, when found, it would release him from loneliness, stupidity, chalk and fear. When he died he was alone, reading, apparently unsatisfied and insensate. He had no money to leave; it had all gone on books. These had been dispatched to us by his landlord, a man who preferred his thoughts rare and slim. The books now provided half the framework for the dinner-scheme, and there had rarely been a sharper, sadder declension of dignity. Bored diners often used the heavier of these books as weapons, and my first act of first-aid was a whiff of ammonia to a boy who had been felled by Frazer's *Golden Bough* while trying to snatch a large slice of apple charlotte, and I am still trying to figure what Frazer would have made of that.

The cooking was done in a minute crypt, a scaly niche. How three women, deliberately chosen on the small side, with their stoves and raw materials could find space in such a galley was a daily miracle. They would stand back to back, making only the smallest chopping movements, and revolving slowly in order to avoid being excessively roasted in any one place. When they fainted that usually meant that the stuff was done. The kitchen remained like a kiln for a good hour after the switching off of the stoves, and on their way home the cooks were often heard to laugh together on an unnaturally high key. They were sometimes thought to be crazy or given to immoral sorts of joking. They were not. They were just cool and glad to be out of that firing chamber.

About the quality of the food I knew nothing. I found the contrast between witless diners and overly pensive books too shocking to the nerves to allow me to eat. My barometer was a boy in one of the far corners. Whenever I saw him catching a peep at *Saint Paul's* between the courses I knew he had been depressed beyond measure. If he picked up *The Drunkard's Dream* he had reached a climax of disgust and had now decided to leave school and go over full-time to depravity.

In 1947 we were given a new dining hall. Even in that mean period there were audible notes of grim inadequacy about this structure. It was prefabricated and was assembled almost as quickly as the first meal. The new kitchen, by comparison with the priest-hole in which the cooks had previously worked, was vast. It was also electrified and the cooks lived in a whirl of instructions. More than once one saw them diligently reading a plate of tart and pouring custard over a handbook. It took them weeks to break the habit of the old fire-dance and resume the type of easy amble natural in kitchens. The dining-hall took a slice out of the rugby field, and until we taught the faster and less observant wings to choose only the softer parts of the building to crash into we had to study methods of getting the best out of concussed players.

The new hall was taken by some as a chance to purge the dinner scheme of the squalor and casualness that had marked the sessions in the library. There was an immediate doubling in the number of diners, and that marked the first step taken by eating towards primacy in the set-up of the school. The old dining-room had been so tiny the boys had to be admitted in small clutches, and even with the limited over-all number the process of feeding them was as slow as a transfusion. In the new place two big sittings saw the multitude replete. For a fortnight after the opening the county meals supervisor threw in what she thought were some gracious details but they were too rich for the blood of the Hogarthian crew who still lived in the stained shadow of the old régime.

'Waiter, this soufflé's uncomfortable.'

Bright tablecloths and pots of flowers created little but confusion among those who thought of school feeding in plain and penitentiary terms. Some tended to regard the flowers as part of the first course and I have yet to find eight boys who can sit around a small table without feeling at once impelled to play the fool with the cloth. They will quietly remove it if only to create a clearer racket with the cutlery.

The reactions of the staff were interesting. There had been no formal act of grace in the old dining-room. The place did not suggest a need for gratitude and when you set eyes on the average platoon of diners in the half-lighted cavern a blessing was the last thing you felt like giving them. In the new place one at least had the sense of a congregation, an occasion. So a proper formula of commencement had to be found. A school with a mossier tradition would have had recourse to some inscrutable bit of Latin, but every splinter of the dynamited nonconformist conscience was represented on the staff, and they wanted things made very plain even at the expense of banality. So masters were told to play it any way they thought fit. One or two of the less obtrusive, who did not want God dragged into a question that affected the rates, just muttered into the gale of diners settling down, and the grace slipped into a pre-Augustine gloom. One or two with sharply anti-dogmatic views couched the grace in a vagueness bordering on code. A few reactionary orators took the chance of appending to the basic religious message some thoughts about Welfare States and dinner schemes, urging boys to eat at home and to force their mams to keep out of factories, and to chew well to avoid the need for dentures which the crazed State would be eager to press on them at fifteen or under. And there was a small group of my colleagues genuinely impressed by the bounty of the County Council, the size of the kitchen, the coloured prints on the wall, showing such events as the landing of the Danes, the knighting of Ralegh, and they kept harping on the theme of miracles until a tapping of spoons from the far corners told them to cut it out and get the potatoes rolling.

The building lost sweetness with a theological haste and finality. The concrete blocks became dirty and discoloured as if mothered by Manchester. Condensation proceeded at the same rate as at Wookey Hole, a wet cave. Slower moving pupils had to be kept wiped and warmed at the first signs of petrifaction. The tables and benches were frail and a whole age away from those ponderous refectories where the fittings were meant to keep the food and diners off the floor. Our benches were collapsible for the convenience of the cleaners and proved it even when the cleaners were nowhere around. Boys got used to eating at swiftly changing levels and conversation never flagged as the angle of the bench-leg switched from nought to ninety.

The appetites of boys vary. There are boys who would barter a cooked dinner for a custard pie any day; boys on whom the smell of cabbage and the sight of meat have some kind of curdling effect. Balancing these lads you have the natural pythons who will scoop all unwanted stuff on to their own plates. I have even seen some of these artists with the food piled up on their plates to the height of one foot, and they do not so much swoop down on it as bore their way through it. There are few things more unsettling than to see a face appear suddenly through a wall of potato. These boys sit through afternoon school, still as stones, their eyes like glazed buttons, their minds at the Pole. On one occasion the Head saw a boy put away so much potato he had him sent to the Pest Officer to be examined for the red and yellow stripes of the Colorado beetle. The boy fainted while trying to keep track of all this irony.

The young, they say, want affection. They

'It's to commemorate the members of the Catering Corps who lost their lives.'

also want gravy. And in our dining-hall they got it. The floor got it as well. Small gravy boats were used and the appointed waiter at each table, also known as a runner, would wear himself out going back and forth to the hatch getting them filled up. The gravy would spill as the runners grew giddy and pools of the stuff would have whole groups of boys with loaded plates figure-skating around the sharper bends while the diners prepared to duck if the plates got out of control. I have rarely seen a set of eaters work so close to the food as that lot. One member of the staff who was against the dinner scheme demanded that we be utterly frank and have the gravy delivered by bucket. Another, a talented mechanic, claimed that he would fit up each table with a gravy-pump. Another emigrated to a robust new country where there was no dinner scheme.

June 1960

Humphrey Lyttelton

WHAT'S FOR PUDDING?

Many years ago, a wartime acquaintance told me a rather indelicate story about an English friend of his who once visited an expensive Parisian brothel. Speaking no French, he ordered at random from a 'menu' of specialities, having no idea what to expect. He was ushered to an upstairs room and left on his own until, after a few minutes, a lady entered, scantily dressed as a waitress and wheeling a well-stocked trolley. Formalities having been exchanged, she proceeded to plaster him where, under the circumstances, he most expected it with whipped cream, trifle and chocolate mousse. At last, crowning the edifice with a maraschino cherry, she announced saucily, 'And now, chéri, I am going to eat eet!' After a moment's contemplation, he waved her aside. 'Oh, no – it looks too good. I think I'll eat it myself.'

I, too, am endowed with a sweet tooth (an apt expression since, alas, one tooth is all you're likely to be left with after a lifetime of indulgence), and I am aware of its drawbacks. As a small boy I very nearly met a premature end eating one of the most delicious desserts I have ever encountered. It was at my grandfather's country seat in Cambridgeshire, where every meal amounted to what would now be regarded as a banquet. The sweet in question was remarkably simple – just a blob of cream whipped to a consistency so light that a suppressed sneeze would have blown it off the plate, and sprinkled with an equally light topping of powdered chocolate. Gasping with delight, I inhaled the chocolate into my windpipe, where it brought all respiratory activity to an abrupt halt. Meals at Babraham Hall were based on the Victorian principle that children should be seen and not heard, so there was no question of drawing attention to myself by jumping up and making asphyxiated noises which would have interrupted the adult conversation. At that stage there hadn't been much of a life to flash before my eyes, but the brief process had begun when a gulp of ginger pop shifted the plug and I lived on to become something of a connoisseur of sweet courses.

Connoisseurship is attained by experiencing the worst as well as the best, and years in boarding-school introduced me to plenty of the former. Tapioca, Semolina and Sago may sound like a Latin American dance team to you, but I recall them as abominations categorised by my late father as 'wet doll stuffing' – revolting in texture, sickly in taste and as enticing to the eye as a bucket of wallpaper adhesive. Fortunately they, along with rice pudding, blancmange and junket, turn out to have been merely facets of the punitive, character-building purposes of boarding-school education, as I have rarely met any of them in adult life. Occasionally I have been reminded of their awful texture, as cold and clammy and unpromising as an executioner's handshake, by a lemon mousse that has lingered too long on a sweet trolley, acquiring a skin thick enough to repel all insults.

And that really brings me to the point of this piece. Most regular eaters-out in Britain could – and probably do – recite in their sleep the contents of the average restaurant sweet trolley. Sherry trifle, Black Forest gâteau, fruit salad, crème caramel, rum baba, mousse – add a cuddly toy and it would be like one of those TV memory games after the umpteenth repeat. It would be disloyal of me to claim that I despise them all. To be honest, my sweet tooth twinges even at the mention of Black Forest gâteau, though it is hard to admire a confection that can't make up its mind whether it belongs to Germany or France. But it's difficult to understand why the selection has dwindled to such boring proportions when there is a whole forgotten world of sweets, desserts and puddings at our disposal.

Did I hear someone scoff at the mention of puddings? Ignore him – he's a day boy, a philistine ensconced beyond civilisation's reach. Anyone brought to maturity via nursery and boarding-school will have a soft spot for puddings, usually overhanging the trouser belt. Let's get our definitions straight. A sweet is so-called simply because it belongs to the sweet (as opposed to savoury) course in a meal. Dessert means much the same thing, the word, from the French, implying that the table will be 'de-served' – in other words, they'll whisk away all the cutlery and condiments, flap the crumbs into your lap with a napkin and clear the decks for what barbarians describe as 'afters'.

'Would you be interested in a backhanded compliment?'

But a pudding is something special. Strictly speaking it should start life as some kind of gooey, finger-clogging dough – indeed, the alternative word 'duff', as in Plum Duff, is a corruption of 'dough'. Baked, boiled or steamed, puddings emerge as a surprisingly wide variety of great names – Queen of Puddings, Jam Roly-Poly, Spotted Dick, Suet Pudding and Treacle, Bread and Butter Puddings which you will never find on a sweet trolley and rarely in a menu. Too stodgy? Well Black Forest Gâteau and sherry trifle, usually covered gratuitously with added cream from a jug, are hardly *nouvelle cuisine*, are they? Too plebeian and 'English'? I am indebted to cookery writer Delia Smith for coming up with a quotation by a seventeenth-century French traveller which puts paid to that canard. 'Ah! What an excellent thing is an English pudding. It is manna that hits the palate of all sorts of people, better than that of the wilderness!'

But I don't want to get bogged down in puddings. There are a lot of other things that can and should be brought in to enliven the present-day sweet course. If English puddings are manna in the wilderness, Fool is the nectar of the gods. I don't know who invented Gooseberry Fool, but they could quite well have had the modern sweet trolley in mind. It's easy to make, will stand about in pots or glasses for any length of time without turning nasty, and has the sort of tart, sharp taste that cleans the palate as thoroughly as any sorbet. And if you want to be even more arcane with very little trouble, there are possets handed down from Elizabethan times which are every bit as light, frothy and tangy as *zabaglione*, and ten times easier to pronounce.

Of course, if you scour the write-ups and study the guide books, you will probably find establishments that offer all these 'afters' as specialities. I can tell you off the top of my head of two places where you can find Bread

'The chef's compliments. You ate with great style and finesse and, with exemplary discretion, put away quite a few jars of the right stuff. You may come again.'

and Butter Pudding, but it won't do you much good. One is the BBC canteen at Broadcasting House, the other the restaurant of the Connaught Hotel in Carlos Place, W1, and the man-in-the-street will find both equally exclusive due to the exigencies of security and economy respectively. (When I win the Pools I shall eat every day at the Connaught, where, in season, they do superb Summer Pudding as well.)

The way to improvement is for us all to start making demands. When a bored waiter offers you Black Forest gâteau, try asking, with an air of surprise, 'Do you not do Mrs Langan's Chocolate Pudding?' If you want to know what that is, go to any of Peter Langan's famed London establishments, from Bistro to Brasserie. It may be the proprietor, rather than just a fly, who lands face down in your soup, but it's worth the risk to experience the greatest addition in modern times to the repertoire of English (or should I say Irish) puddings. Sorry, I've got to go – my sweet tooth is giving me gyp and I think there's some Marmalade Pudding in the fridge.

July 1986

David Taylor

talks to

ALBERT ROUX

For us now perhaps a glass of bub. I must excuse him for one moment because the telephone sounds, but afterwards we begin to talk of many things, which he does not so often do in the press. It is as a rule his big brother, Michel you know, who does prefer to do the talking. For Monsieur Albert, privacy is a sacred thing, but today we make an exception. So.

We are as a matter of fact next door to Le Gavroche. In 1967 he has started this restaurant, in the heart of Mayfair where he likes very much to be, and today we talk next door in 47 Park Street, which is a very special house to stay, we don't call it an hotel, and is now where he makes an office. Much has changed since he and Michel began at Le Gavroche to work together for the first time, and he remembers they used to cook together by day, then in the evening Michel remained at the stove whilst he, Albert, took the orders because only he understood what they were saying in English. Afterwards they began also Le Poulbot and Le Gamin, The Waterside Inn and Gavvers and felt of each as if they were their children to be cherished, you know. Today, of course, all these have become revolutionised, he would say.

Well, because it is true today that he is very much a businessman and an entrepreneur, as well as in his heart the chef. Perhaps we can say it was always so, because even when he was a young person at school in Semur-en-Brionnais, which is I know Saône et Loire, where he was born in the middle of wartime in 1941, then already he used to trade in marbles or whatever and knew perhaps that one day he would do business. It is very important for us to begin at the beginning, in so far as whatever has happened to him and his brother since, a lot as a matter of fact, they must never forget that once it was a very humble beginning, which will always be inside him for as long as he dies.

His first taste of working with food, then, was during his apprenticeship at the Pâtisserie Leclerc, in St Mande I know, until he spent one year further at the Pâtisserie Bras République in Paris, before first coming to London which was a revelation. Still today, I know, he has a French passport, but his heart is now British for many years. But when first he has come to London, Monsieur Albert was at the Embassy of France, then Lady Astor as her chef and later on he served with Sir Charles Clore which was very, very different, until at last he was able to set up on his own right. This was of course as a restaurateur, although nowadays he is reverting to the role of entrepreneur much more, as we have said.

You know it is very nice to do both things. He enjoys most of all to cook, of course. He enjoys most of all to be inside his kitchen. Of course, he must come outside in the room

to meet the customers, but that is a role which Michel prefers more than him and as a matter of fact, if customers should ask Monsieur Albert to sit down and join them for a drink, he automatically declines and prefers to return into the kitchen.

To be honest with me, he would say that at Le Gavroche, he is not cooking for the customers. No. He is cooking for himself. If they don't like it, then he is very sorry. He is very sorry if they don't like the way he has done something, but he is not going to change it. It is, after all, a three-star restaurant there, the only other besides The Waterside Inn as is well known, but it is not so everywhere.

It is not so, for example, at Rouxl Brittania, where he has begun to experiment in the City with *sous vide*, which we can call boil-in-the-bag if we wish. At Rouxl Britannia, the opportunity was begun to transform everyday eating, by using the finest ingredients pre-prepared at the source, until at the restaurant they are re-heated to be served. For this to work as a success there was very much work to be done, which he has done almost as a scientist, I know, investigating all sorts of methods including irradiation of foodstuffs. Today at Rouxl Britannia (which is a name which appeals very much to his sense of humour these days) they are serving 1,800 meals each week and we can say that it has become a sucess, although it is not yet open for one year. The results now are analysed by computer and in such a place he would change to meet the requirements of customers much more. It is very much a matter of feeling. It is a matter of whether such and such a thing feels right. Sometimes at first the things did not come out right, you know, but now the idea of *sous vide* has taken him by the neck, he would say.

I should understand that his prime objective is at all times to have enjoyment in what he does. Yes. You should not touch anything in life for the money alone. You know he has always remembered, from when he was working with Sir Charles Clore, that he found a very rich man, but he did not find at all a very happy man. He was a man who was tormented. He was a man who feared always that one day he would be poor again. He could be a very generous man. One day he gave to Albert an envelope full of money, which he did not have to do. But then another day he could be a very mean man. Some days, you know, he would come in and inspect the fridge to see what it contained. It was quite a change for the young Albert to be working for such a person, where before always he had worked for blue-bloods. There would be a book to be written about such days, but he absolutely will not. What went on in those days was private and that is absolutely sacred for them, as now it is also for him.

When at the end of the week, for example, he gets home. During the week he will be in 47 Park Street or in Chelsea, but at the end

'Just sits there toying with her food.'

of the week he will be in the countryside in Petworth, West Sussex, where he has made his home with his wife and children. There are two. And I know he has been so lucky to have a son and a daughter, now also a son-in-law, who are working in the business, but of their own choice. Not of his choice, so to speak, but because they themselves want to. It is a very special home to him, with 13 acres of garden which he likes very much to cultivate, with his dogs and his goat, most of all the opportunity to go fishing, which he likes to do very much all over the world. For some other things, it is a great pleasure to listen to some classical music, to listen to opera or to go to Glyndebourne which he does many times a year, or to go to the ballet best of all. As to the objects, he would say that he likes oil paintings very much, but in art it always should be a matter of what you see and not what you pay.

Which reminds him now of one time he was making a birthday cake for Sir Winston Churchill, and he was called in from the kitchen, and there was placed a glass of bub for him, until Sir Winston turned to him and he said, 'Chef, you made here a work of art, you know. The only difference there is between this cake and the paintings on this wall, we are now going to cut this cake and to eat it and tomorrow it is a forgotten thing.' This was extremely true, you know. Just the other day, the French government declared that cooking was an art, but the fact remains that a chef is only as good as his last meal. The next day he must start all over again.

Certainly that is it. That is an incentive or challenge we can say. And you know that in this country we are seeing a revolution. There is much more excitement in Britain now than he would say in France. It is the young chefs here who are showing the world what they can do. And not only in the business, but every day the telephone sounds and

'Is the boeuf Stroganoff available in another colour?'

someone is saying, 'Monsieur Albert! I have made this quite fantastic elderberry syrup, or whatever it might be, and you must now taste it!' Many times he has been told of things which turn out to be fantastic. There is such enthusiasm everywhere. He will call a cab some days and the driver will recognise him and talk about the book (*New Classic Cuisine*) or what he is making for dinner. It is quite fantastic and now you see in the foreign papers about Britain, or here at the 47 Park Street where everyone comes, royalty, or politicians, or big stars, and say to him that it is fantastic, which everyone of course likes to hear very much. It is a sobering thought, for another example, that *New Classic Cuisine* has sold over 100,000 copies,

which he did not expect, although Michel said it would, maybe because he wrote it, you know.

We must now finish off the bub and tour the kitchens in Le Gavroche for one moment to confirm that all is well, look at what is what. It is, of course, very much busy. And today especially, when he has a chef on holiday and has therefore had to roll up his own sleeves and step in to what he still loves doing the best. The telephone sounds an ultimate time and it is a person who wants to do a deal with him to make a huge hotel somewhere else. It must wait. He is needed in the kitchens and so must say goodbye.

July 1987

'*Remember our first meal together, when we sat on soap-boxes and ate off a tea-chest?*'

'Ronald and I have discovered this marvellous little bistro just around the corner.
We often mispronounce everything and they never seem to mind.'

'Don't go to any trouble on my account. I'll just have what everybody else is having.'

'Yes, I come here a lot – you'll find the trout all know me.'

'Eat it while it's still £10.50.'

Alan Coren

TWO SLEEPY PEOPLE, WITH NOTHING TO DO

The English are not a sensual nation: puritanism, a cold climate, and an education which frowns on joy have seen to that. They go to bed with each other for various reasons, but only sometimes for the simple pleasure of food. They go there in order to be seen by other people; to have their egos massaged by subservient waiters; to impress the opposite sex with their social adroitness; to get drunk.

Tatler

It was generally agreed to have been the most super wedding one had ever been to.

The bride, of course, looked absolutely stunning.

'Doesn't Lucinda look absolutely stunning?' said her best friend Melissa.

'*Rather!*' cried Melissa's husband.

'Jolly stately and serene,' said Melissa, as Lucinda swept past them down the aisle on the arm of the Earl. 'One is rather reminded of old Queen Mary, isn't one?'

'I thought that had three funnels,' said Melissa's husband, frowning.

Rodney-Rodney made a magnificent bridegroom. Scion of the only English family allowed to hyphenate its Christian names (a favour bestowed at Bannockburn when one of Rodney-Rodney's illustrious ancestors had relieved a pustule on Edward II), he was as tall as it is possible to be without arousing genetic suspicion, and slim as a flute. True, his chin fell away sharply from his upper canines, above which, as if in Dame Nature's kindly compensation, his nose sprang out for several overstated inches (he had been known as Beaky-Beaky at Dame Poumfret's Preparatory Academy for the Appallingly Dim, and the name had stuck); but by great good fortune, his bride's county nose was retroussé to the point of invisibility and her chin jutted out so far that her small bust lay in permanent shadow. In short, Lucinda and Rodney-Rodney appeared to complement one another perfectly: when they kissed at the altar, their two profiles meshed as effortlessly as Bentley clutch-plates.

It was, however, the first kiss in which either of them had ever been involved. Throughout her twenty-one years, Lucinda's only romantic attachment had been a heavy crush on Red Rum, while Rodney-Rodney, at twenty-three, had entered into only one non-platonic relationship, with a Fräulein Sharon, to whose discreet Curzon Street premises he would repair every Thursday after the Brigade dinner, to be beaten with a blancoed length of Boer webbing.

But because Lucinda's daddy, the Earl, owned eighty thousand acres of shooting but preferred fishing, whereas Rodney-Rodney's daddy, Charlie-Charlie, owned eighty miles of salmon-river but preferred shooting, their marriage had been a foregone conclusion for some time.

Nevertheless, to say that they were ill-prepared is seriously to underestimate the English upper classes: on the day before the ceremony, Charlie-Charlie took Rodney-Rodney into the library at Toppins, gave him a large brandy, and showed him an illustrated copy of Fernleigh's *Breeding Springers*; and the Countess, for her part, formally handed over to Lucinda the Hapsburg bullet upon which her family's brides had been biting ever since the Thirty Years' War.

At the reception, everybody got wonderfully, wonderfully tight. They danced the

*'Trust you to spoil it all!
One sip of champagne and you treat me
like a sex object.'*

tiny paddling-pool beside the loo so that her rubber duck could float about without getting lonely. She unpacked carefully, put her bullet by the bed, and slid between the sheets, leaving Rodney-Rodney to pad into the bathroom with *Breeding Springers* for a little last-minute revision while she turned the pages of *Tatler*, which was the only reading-matter she ever saw and from which she invariably took her behavioural cues.

It was while flicking through the glossy breathlessness in the hope of finding, perhaps, some indication of when the bullet was supposed to be enmouthed, that she suddenly issued a shrill cry. Rodney-Rodney, who had been barking seductively behind the door, dashed out, his long face twisted apprehensively at this new evidence of feminine unpredictability.

'What is it, old stick?' he cried. 'Not women's problems?' He raked, gamely, through his sparse garnering of marital notes. 'Should I burp you, or something?'

'Oh, Beaky-Beaky!' cried Lucinda, eyes a-

Lancers, in which seven shoulders were dislocated, and the Gay Gordons, in which no fewer than thirty-seven people made the same joke about MI5, and an Eightsome Reel, in which no fewer than thirty-seven people made the same joke about Highland underwear, and they played Maim the Staff, in which Rodney-Rodney himself managed to disable two footmen and an under-gardener with Dom Perignon bottles from sixty paces, despite having had his monocle shattered during the Ladies Excuse-Me Wall Game.

And at six o'clock, being tired little teddy bears, the happy couple slipped away in Rodney-Rodney's Lagonda across the croquet lawn, and, pausing only to leave the offside front wing on an elderly yew, purred off towards the far Savoy and the first leg of their mooners in Canners.

It was a pleasant suite: by jumping on the bed, Rodney-Rodney found he could bang his head on the ceiling, and Lucinda was ecstatic to find that there was even a tiny,

'You like the chicken soup?'

shine, 'Nothing like that! There is a super piece in *Tatler* about how people are supposed to do it!'

'Do what?'

'You know,' murmured Lucinda. 'Thing.'

'*Thing*?' exclaimed Rodney-Rodney, his imperceptible jaw dropping. 'In *Tatters*?'

'Isn't it thrilling?' shouted Lucinda.

'And just in the nick of, er, whateveritis!' cried Rodney-Rodney, jumping up and down. 'Does it tell one how to examine one's feet for hardpad? This book's jolly difficult to follow.'

'There's nothing about that here,' replied Lucinda. 'Apparently one sometimes starts off with food.'

'Hurrah!' shouted Rodney-Rodney. 'I think this ought to be one of those times, don't you? One works up a jolly enormous appetite barking, I can tell you! Hardly surprising dogs get right down to it, shoving their beezers in the jellymeat, no knives or forks or anything, one suddenly sees the reason behind it. Let's have some oysters and a duck or two!'

'Right-ho!' shrieked his bride, clapping her hands. 'I say, Beaky-Beaky, I was never allowed to eat in bed, were you? Isn't it absolutely super being grown-up? And the other thing about getting food sent up is the waiters will be able to massage our egos!'

Two lines crinkled on Rodney-Rodney's teeny brow.

'What on earth are *those*?' he said. 'I say, I hope it's not that thing they caught little Berkshire doing with Crown Prince Bhunah at Dame Poumfret's. If one went blind, one's hunting career would be utterly ruined!'

'It'll be all right,' said Lucinda confidently. 'There'll be other people watching.'

'What sort of people?'

'It doesn't say. I should think any old people would do. Why don't I order the food while you nip out and whip in a few spectators?'

'*Super!*' cried Rodney-Rodney, slipping into his dressing-gown. 'I say, old thing, is one allowed to drink, too?'

'It says,' replied Lucinda, scanning the page almost without moving her lips, 'that one is supposed to get drunk!'

Rodney-Rodney reeled.

'What bliss!' he shouted. 'Is it any wonder one's parents keep one in the old harry darkers about thing? One would never do anything else!'

When, ten minutes later, he returned, there were five small Japanese businessmen with him. They bowed towards Lucinda.

'Best I could do, I'm afraid,' said Rodney-Rodney. 'They were jabbering in the corridor. They don't seem to speak anything but Jap, but they shot off like grouse when I snapped my fingers. Can't think why. Do you suppose they're prisoners-of-war, or something?'

'Jolly lucky being imprisoned in the Savoy,' said Lucinda.

'Oh, I don't know.' said Rodney-Rodney. 'I bet they have to stick to the set menu. Things like that. Will they do?'

'I should think so,' replied Lucinda, waving the Japanese to sit. 'They only have to watch, after all.'

There was a soft knock on the door, and Rodney-Rodney opened it to admit two waiters pushing a trolley, and a sommelier with a shouldered crate of Bollinger. He shot into bed. They followed with the trolley, served the oysters, eased a cork, and were about to leave, when Rodney-Rodney cried:

'I say, would you mind staying? This is our wedding-night.'

The trio paused; but since Rodney-Rodney's accent was full of money, they stayed, sliding themselves professionally back against the walls. Lucinda, having despatched three bivalves with scarcely a slurp, hurled the shells at the gazing Japs. She hit two.

'I say!' exclaimed her husband. 'That's a bit strong, old girl. Geneva Convention and all that.'

'One is supposed,' replied Lucinda, passing the magazine across, 'to impress the opposite sex with one's social adroitness.'

'I *see!*' shouted Rodney-Rodney. 'Well, I'm jolly impressed, old girl. I've not seen better chucking from a sitting position since Farty Cork-Snettering laid out the Connaught's maitre d' with a chump chop! Still, just to show that one is no mean hand oneself when the social adroitness rosettes are being dished out ... '

Whereupon Rodney-Rodney sprang lithely from the bed, scattering croquettes, stood on his head in the middle of the room, and downed an entire bottle of champagne without taking it from his inverted lips.

'As performed on Boat Race Night '74!' he shrieked.

The Japanese applauded.

'God,' gasped Rodney-Rodney, when he had removed his head from the waste-bin and allowed a little colour to drain back into his saffron cheeks, 'isn't this the most super fun? Beats being a springer, I can tell you!' He wiped his mouth, while a clench-faced waiter took the waste-bin to the bathroom. 'What do we have to do next?'

There was no reply.

Rodney-Rodney loped erratically to the bed. Lucinda, having drunk two bottles on her own loyal behalf, lay fast asleep, her head on a duck, her auburn locks fetchingly highlighted by the *sauce de cerises.*

Her husband gazed at her for some time, rocking on his bare heels.

'Was it wonderful for you, too, old thing?' he murmured finally.

Then he sat down sharply on the floor beside her, and opened his third bottle.

Back at the grimy composing-room of *Tatler,* the horny-handed printers toasted their latest brilliant sabotage in Newcastle Brown, and plotted their next. They had been given a riding article to set, explaining how best to present a horse at a 6-foot jump. It would be the work of a moment to make it 16-foot. By such canny sleights, a dropped line here, a transposed word there, it would not be long, surely, before all the ancient lines died out, all the ensigns of privilege were extirpated, and the revolution was quietly ushered in.

January 1980

Clement Freud

A RECIPE FOR SEDUCTION

I used to pity my school friends who went into the Army or the City for their inability to combine work with love. I was a romantic . . . and became an apprentice cook.

My friends would find girls, take them out and bore them to distraction holding forth on subjects as compelling as .303 rifles; 'with profits' policies, or deposit accounts. They would then complain about the girl's early departure home.

I found no girls, mainly because I worked what would now be called 'unsociable hours', but I was pretty certain that when I did, my growing experience with pots and pipkins would achieve very much more than did their mundane small talk.

Admittedly, having intended to learn to do irresistible things with white truffles, partridge breasts, plovers' eggs and grape brandy, the wartime economy confined my culinary forays to sago, coley – which is an off-white fish – and margarine – about the only things that were not in short supply. But we of check trousers and proudly starched hats did with sago, coley and margarine things that had never before been attempted

'Waste of time, these fire drills.'

with those journeyman products; what is more, we did these things using the most eclectic utensils, from copper pans to French vegetable knives, not to mention sauteuses, mandolines, tammy cloths and pallets.

My first encounter with a real girl (a description which excluded sisters of school friends) was at a Christmas staff party. I forget her name, but remember that she worked in the linen room, was tall, thin and lived a very long way from a Tube station. I walked her home from the staff party and when we got to her house, she leaned down and I tried to kiss her mouth; I got her chin.

It seemed a disaster at the time, but on reflection it was not too bad for a first attempt. Certainly the girl was quite impressed, mentioning that she had never had anyone kiss her chin. The walk back seemed shorter.

I spent a lot of time and energy on that girl over the next few weeks, and realising that compulsive food was unavailable, other food unappetising, decided that drink would be my best chance of transforming her into something other than a tall, thin, distant and mildly bored recipient of a chin-peck. I read books in the library, but was steadily frustrated by maddening phrases such as 'also a suspicion of oriental roots' or 'then a few hours maceration in Mediterranean spices.'

One night I tried it with gin. I showed her that there was nothing remotely suspicious about a young man of good family and dishonourable intentions giving a girl gin by drinking a glass or two myself . . . and passed out.

I never saw the linen room girl again . . . but the idea of a love potion to aid my romantic desires became increasingly attractive. Some inexpensive, easily obtainable concoction that would transform a cool collected female into a hot, frenzied, passionate octopus (I was looking only at the short term). In that seventeenth year of my life, I spent the days cooking wartime food, messing around with coley and sago and seeing what the odd bottle-ends of Moselle that came down from the restaurant would do for me.

In my state it was hard to tell. My thoughts were so deeply wrapped up in the expectation of love that any food or drink, or lack thereof, made me feel as I would have had my victim feel.

About a month after the gin episode, I heard on the grapevine that a liftboy called Wrackham had a sister – and knowing what sort of a chap Wrackham was, there seemed every likelihood that Miss Wrackham might be the very person I was looking for. By that time I had a room in South Terrace with a gas ring. I took Miss Wrackham to a film and brought her home for 'supper'.

All was carefully and lovingly arranged; 'all' included a concoction described in a book by Norman Douglas which had lured a page-boy in a Berlin hotel into the most enjoyable *halbe stunde*. Hock and Seltzer with a slug of Apricot Brandy served in a tall frosted glass, the rim rubbed with lemon peel and dried with caster sugar.

I offered to hang up Miss Wrackham's coat but she said it was all right and sat on the bed.

I cooked two fillets of coley on a bed of sago and she asked whether there were no chips; there were no chips. The conversation lapsed and I looked deep into her eyes and said, 'I think I have something that will please you very much,' went out and brought in the frosted glasses of prepared Hock and Apricot Brandy freshly topped with Seltzer.

No book ever gives you the timing of a love potion. Should it take effect as the liquor touches the lining of the stomach, or does it, like aspirins, take 20 minutes? I drank my glass and sat watching her for signs as she sipped bird-like from hers. It took less time than aspirins; to the best of my memory, about eight minutes, and if it was not all passion and tentacles, it was a very fair manifestation of acquiescence.

Later that evening, I offered her another glass and she said no, thanks, she must be going. I saw her to South Ken tube station, feeling like a satiated roué.

It was not until several weeks later, when I had irrevocably unbalanced my budget with wild purchases of Apricot Brandy, that I learnt from diverse colleagues that Miss Wrackham also performed on half pints of mild ale.

In fact, my former schoolfriends would probably have bowled her over with accounts of cleaning cap badges.

June 1975

'Which one of you has been fooling around with the place-cards?'

Ernest Jenkins

THE GOURMETS

The conversation had, as usual, come round to food and restaurants; but new plays and new books having had their turn, you must not be in too much of a hurry to accuse us of sheer blatant materialism. The discussion took its usual course, beginning with laments as to the decline of this and that renowned restaurant, and passing to the merits of the smaller recent enterprises of ex-head waiters, whether in Soho or the West-End. With familiarity we named these proprietors. Antoine here, Philippe there, Emilio somewhere else; all these astute, smiling, bowing foreigners who conquer London by way of the œsophagus – who, in short, feed the brute – our references to them carrying a suggestion of intimacy nearer and dearer than that rendered to our own kith and kin.

Each of course had his speciality, his masterpiece. Antoine's *bœuf à la mode* was alleged to be mated to an even better sauce than you get at that place in Paris. Fifteen ingredients, if you please, with a very good port – not cooking – as one of them. Philippe, it seems, gets his hams no one knows where – he won't divulge – but they are marvellous. All in the curing, of course; sugar and saltpetre rubbed in, don't you know, and the special secret wood to make the right smoke.

'Now that's what beats me,' said Morrison angrily, 'why a foreigner should be able to get a better ham than I can. Heaven knows I've tried hard enough, and the beggar won't tell, won't he? Monstrous!'

Emilio's particular triumph seems to be his way of stuffing veal; and so we went on, naming our table preferences and elaborating our delight in them like so many Brillat-Savarins.

Up to this time the General had not spoken, but now he broke in, on the top of a peculiarly succulent eulogy of *canard à la presse* from our hostess.

'Have a little pity!' he cried. 'Here you all are, exploiting your favourite greedinesses, without giving a thought to those whose appetite has gone for ever. How you can go on enjoying your food like this I can't understand. Don't you ever get tired of eating? Don't you ever regret the money you pay out to these artful aliens? Although now I want nothing at all – a piece of toast and some fruit – I've tasted the choicest dishes of every country in the world, and what has been surprising me during all this greedy gourmandising chatter is the total absence of any reference to the best food, the best flavours of all: the food we have all liked – at any rate the men here – better than anything we have ever eaten, and should not resent if we found nothing else laid out for us on the table. You may crack up your *bœuf à la mode*, your pressed duck with orange salad, your *bécasse flambée*, your *perdreaux aux choux*, your *coq en pâte*, your *poularde truffée*, in fact any of your old messes of the *maison*, but I'll bet that, if he's honest, there's not a man in this room who won't have to admit that none

of these things has given his palate such pleasure, caused it such excitement, as the simple, unassuming but enchanting article of diet I am going to name.'

He paused and looked round at us one by one.

'Be honest now,' he said.

'Of course,' we replied.

'Very well, then: potted meat.'

A sigh of acquiescence broke from the whole company.

'Of course,' we said again. 'Why, yes – potted meat. Nothing like it.'

We became ruminative. As for myself, with the inward eye I visualised again across the years a small cylinder of tin covered with a shiny buff paper, and on the paper the magic words 'Turkey and Tongue.'

'Then I was right?' the General asked.

'Absolutely,' someone said. 'My own choice was Bloater Paste.'

'But Anchovy lasted longer,' said another. 'Being stronger, you spread it thinner.'

'What about Chicken and Ham?' asked the General.

'Don't disturb Sir Roger. He's fermenting.'

'And then,' said our hostess, 'there was the potted beef made at home, in an oval white china pot, with a rich yellow paste on the top. We were always told not to eat this paste.'

'But you did?' the General inquired.

'Of course,' said our hostess. 'At least I did. You seem to think, General, that passion for potted meat belongs exclusively to your own sex, but, so far as I am concerned, you're wrong. In fact I can remember how, without being in the least a Suffragette, I always felt slighted by the fact that that divine stuff in tooth-paste pots was called 'Gentleman's Relish.' Why for gentlemen only? It's decided me to take the hint you dropped and give a surprise dinner-party where there's nothing but potted things.'

'Perfectly safe,' said the General. 'Not a soul would be disappointed.'

'I'll do it,' said our hostess; 'but no one shall know about it beforehand. And the piece de résistance shall be a very special mixture which my cook and I will devise for the occasion, and which by way of a mild revenge we'll call 'Lady's Relish.' Will you come?'

We accepted nem. con.   E.V.L.

September 1929

John Arlott

WHEN THE SPIRIT MOVES

The word brandy covers a multitude of drinks and is subject to as many misconceptions. It is just to say that brandy is the finest of spirits; and cognac the finest of brandies, approached only – a few would claim, matched – by armagnac from a few kilometres further south in France.

Strictly speaking, brandy is distilled wine: but the term is also used of many kinds of distilled fruit juices; notably Applejack and Calvados, both made from apple juice; marc (from grape pulp) and distillates of fruit, most impressively, the *eaux de vie* or *alcools blancs* of Alsace – such as quetsch, made from blue plums, fraise (strawberries), kirsch (cherries), mirabelle (yellow plums), enzian (yellow gentian), reineclaude (greengages), framboise (raspberries), houx (holly berries).

True brandy (the name comes from the Dutch *brandewijn* or burnt wine), though, is distilled from grape wine. While all cognac is brandy, only a relatively small proportion even of French brandy is cognac: while on a world scale, California alone produces more brandy than all France. There is a Spanish brandy which, at its rare best, is extremely fine; most of it, though, is blandly indistinguished; Greece, Germany, Italy, South Africa, Cyprus and Russia all make measurable quantities of brandy and virtually every wine-producing country distils some. The proportion is a matter of economics; it takes nine gallons of wine to make a gallon of brandy, which would rarely be viable in a fine wine area.

Over the centuries, brandy became a commodity: it was popular with smugglers for the good reasons that its name was known, it contained a large proportion of alcohol per keg; and because cognac and armagnac were accepted as luxury drinks. In Alderney, the smuggling of brandy to Britain became a major part of the island's revenue. In 1823 one of the jurats (magistrates) told the historian of the Channel Islands, John Jacob, that his expenditure on shipping such contraband was over £50,000 a year; small wonder huge fortunes were made; and appreciable damage was done to its economy when, in 1808, the British government took serious steps to stop the traffic. Both there and elsewhere some claim it continues; but now high-money contraband consists in drugs, where the profits, like the risks, are so much greater. Looking back, although the smuggling of brandy was fraught with peril, it has an aura of romance.

Nowadays, the competition is commercial; substantially between cognac and 'other brandies': on the factual and publicity arguments of sheer quality, cognac walks away from the opposition. Britain, for example, on recent figures, imports about 15 million bottles a year against 13 million of 'others'. Cognac consumption has increased all over the world. The last figures showed the United States leading the world league with 28 million bottles annually; then came Great Britain, 17 million; France was third with a domestic consumption of over 11 million, with West Germany slightly less and then, more surprisingly, Hong Kong, 8 million, followed by Japan, the latest entrant to the highest lists, with 7 million.

The laws of cognac allow the addition of distilled water to bring the spirit down to the legal level, of caramel to colour the otherwise colourless liquid, and an infusion of oak chips to reinforce the impression of wood-age. The final quality depends upon, firstly, the character and standard of the basic fermented wine from which it is distilled; the extent and fashion of the distillation; whether or not it is subsequently rectified; the skill and the resources of the blender, the kind of cask and the humidity of the cellar in which it is matured; and the length of that process.

The making of cognac, and even the use of its name, is most strictly legally controlled. It may be made only in the traditional, huge, onion-shaped, copper pot-stills, and from eight types of grapes; ideally the *folle blanche* and *colombard*; grown in the precisely defined region of Charente and Charente Maritime, which is, in its turn, subdivided into districts producing seven different grades of wine, from *grande* and *petite champagne* which make the finest blend (because of the chalk in which the vines are grown). It is then matured in casks of oak from the nearby forests of Limousin or Tronçais – usually in the attics of Cognac. There it may improve for, it is said, as much as fifty years, requiring constant 'refreshing' to make good the loss by evaporation which, over the ages, has cloaked the neighbouring roofs and walls with the black, velvety, fungoid deposit called 'The Angels' Share' – and at a cost to the trade put at over 15 million bottles a year. Once bottled it ceases to improve.

Cognac is pre-eminent among brandies primarily because of the suitability of the local wine for distilling; and secondly for the immense stock-resources of the great blending houses. Brandy, even cognac, varies between the splendid and the indifferent: even the same of different age. There are few hard and fast rules about cognac; some great houses blend after maturing; others blend first; some do not blend at all, but produce single vineyard cognacs of considerable distinction. One of the finest houses considers it maintains its high standard by blending as many as seven different *grande champagne* brandies of an average age of twenty years.

The French have clear-mindedly renounced the idea of 'vintage cognac' – though some few bottles may still exist in Britain. The existence of a 'Napoleon' (1812) brandy – what Cyril Ray has called 'The Napoleon Legend' – is, of course, virtually impossible. After even 70 years – leave alone 170 – in cask it would have had to be topped up so often that the original spirit would be diluted as to be practically non-existent; while in bottle it would simply have faded to a ghost of its original self.

A truly fine cognac is complex, warming, subtle, deep, vigorous but graceful, distinguished and satisfying; indeed, the best could even be described as profound. As cognacs differ, so do drinkers' palates. Probably the wisest course is to ask wine merchants of integrity – or trusted wine waiters – what they would recommend; and then go on tasting their recommendations until the right one turns up.

French law registers cognac in eight age-stages or, in the case of a blend, that of the youngest, in *comptes*, from oo in their first year to 6 – the maximum – for those more than six years old. The minimum age at which brandy may be sold in France is one year; but in Britain it is three.

Drink it, at best, in a tulip-shaped, thin-walled glass of modest size; and warm it in the cupped hand; the goldfish-bowl size, heated at a flame, is a useless affectation. Do not hurry; simply sniff it first; the aroma of a really fine cognac, reasonably pondered, can emerge as infinitely complex and beguiling. As the warmth comes through, sip it slowly. The first mouthful may be extremely small, yet flood the palate – and beyond – with flavour. Mix it if you must; but that is sacrilege in the case of a fine cognac. As Charles Lamb once remarked, 'A mixture of brandy and water spoils two good things.'

The matter of using brandy in cooking is too extensive to detail; but cognac in particular is called for in dishes involving fish, shellfish, salads, meat – especially steak – game, ices, cakes as well as 'coffees'. Fruits in brandy, too, are popular – plums, chestnuts, raspberries and Monsieur Breton's variety of *confits*. There are many side-products of both brandy and cognac; the almost countless *eaux de vie*, many cocktails, and cognac-based liqueurs which, by French law, must

A HOME TRUTH
Host (sotto voce). 'IS THIS THE *BEST* CLARET, MARY?'. *Mary (audibly)*.
'IT'S THE BEST YOU'VE *GOT*, SIR!'

indicate the extent of cognac – only – by the description '*au cognac*' (a minimum of 30% but may also contain neutral spirit); '*à base de cognac*' (at least 50%), and *exclusivement au cognac*, or *de cognac* (at least 100% cognac base). Probably the most popular of the cognac-based liqueurs is Grand Marnier; others well liked in Charentes are Sa'ala and Sève Patricia: while an American firm sells a pleasing mixture of brandy and Benedictine.

One of the most popular drinks in the cognac area is Pineau de Charentes, made originally, it is said, by an accident; which arrests the fermentation of the local grape juice by the addition of brandy: it is sweet, strong (18%–22% of alcohol) and fruity. Protected since 1935 by *appellation contrôlée*, its popularity has spread in recent years far beyond the area of its production; and it drinks all too easily.

Brandy is also a stimulant and a rectifier. When George IV – then Prince of Wales – first met his bride-to-be, Caroline of Brunswick, in 1794, he received her courteously, then turning to the nobleman who had escorted her from Brunswick – 'Malmesbury, I am not well: pray bring me a glass of brandy.'

July 1987

or black ants – brandy it was, if called brandy and if it resembled brandy in taste, colour and smell.]

(*With apologies to W. S. Gilbert*)
If you want a receipt for the liquor called brandy,
Known to the world as 'Imported from France,'
Take some potatoes – or anything handy –
The very first thing that encounters your glance:
Figs decomposing (O, sweet putrefaction!
Devised for the cheap distillation of wine!);
Ants or cockroaches, disabled in action,
Or wasting away in a rapid decline;
Maize that is damaged and meant for manuring,
Rye with the dry-rot, and unfit for food,
Fish that is tainted, and useless for curing,
Sawdust a handful, a foot of charred wood;
Squeeze from these elements all that is squeezable
(The process is easy, simple and feasible),
And the wash you produce, if in colour and smell
It resembles pure brandy, is ready to – *sell*.

August 1903

F.L. Greig

SCOTCH BRANDY

[In a prosecution under the Sale of Food and Drugs Act, at the instance of the Lanark County authorities, against a Glasgow firm of purveyors, for selling adulterated brandy, some useful information was recently obtained. Commercial witnesses contended that, no matter what the origin of spirit was – whether grapes, grain, rotten figs, potatoes,

'Me, too – I believe it's better to travel drunkenly than to arrive . . .'

'You know the rules, Mr. Johnston – no wine making!'

James Ainsworth

OVER A BARREL

How do you make the best wine in the world?

Raoul Blondin, the agile octogenarian *maître de chai* at Château Mouton-Rothschild, hopped from one leg to the other as he leant back against a railing and surveyed the one thousand brand new casks full of the 1984 vintage. 'Good soil, good grapes, plenty of sun, and a good *maître de chai*,' he said in perfect French, ticking off the first three on his fingers and timing a shrug and a smile for the fourth.

Is that all, I wondered to myself in English, and would in due course have put the question aloud in his own language for M. Blondin's benefit, had he not nimbly forestalled it: '*C'est tout.*'

But for many people *c'est* quite obviously not *tout* at all.

There seem to be two stony types from whom it is difficult to extract the bloody details of how they go about making wine. Those at the top end make such indisputably fine and sought-after stuff that they have no need to brag about it; those at the other end are afraid that their thoroughly disreputable practices will be found out. In between, most people will bore the pants off you if you let them.

I am not qualified to pronounce on whether Château Mouton-Rothschild makes the best wine in the world, but Bordeaux châteaux do not get kicked upstairs to the first growths, as Mouton did in 1973, without having something really big going for them. The really big thing it has had going for it, apart from the wine, is Baron Philippe Rothschild.

When the Médoc league table was drawn up in 1855, the operational definition of status was based on the prices the wines had been fetching for some time before that, and Mouton's relatively recent rise to fame put it not in the First, but at the top of the Second division. Baron Philippe took charge in 1922 at the age of 21 and was determined to rectify the mistake. The wines have for long had parity with first growth prices, and there are few, if any, who would quibble with its right to be numbered among the top few wines on the planet. The Baron is thus captain of the only team to gain promotion in 130 years of the game.

Although Raoul Blondin now concerns himself more with cellarmasterly duties such as selecting the Baron's wines for dinner, or showing visitors around the impressive *chai* and fine museum, he must take a chunk of the credit for having put in 50 years' work that led up to this unique elevation. His guiding principle, he says, is to maintain the old traditions. As the Baron put it succinctly in motto form after successfully achieving his upward mobility penetration situation:

Premier je suis	First I am
Second je fus	Second I was
Mouton ne	Mouton doesn't
change	change

'*Another Saturday night and still no one's invented alcohol!*'

'She's much too la-di-da for the likes of us.'

In the cellars there is no sign of stainless steel, no glass-lined cement vats, no epoxy resin containers. Tradition is enshrined in wood, for both fermenting the wine and maturing it. Few sights are more dramatic for the man with half a dozen bottles in a rack under the stairs than to see the doors swing open to reveal the first year *chai*. The one thousand casks each holding 225 litres are expansively displayed in a single layer, purple-stained around the centre between the metal hoops, where the young wine has slopped over as the barrel was filled. There's no fun in being a baron unless you can throw money around, so Mouton treats itself to new ones every year, made from Limousin oak, costing 2,000 francs apiece. A cheque for the equivalent of £170,000 goes off to the cooper's and what have you got to show for it? Not much until the wine is sold, where-upon 60 pee a bottle will go back into the tin marked 'next year's barrel fund'.

M. Blondin is probably right about the sun and the grapes, and he is surely on firm ground when referring to the soil: it supports not only the vines but the whole edifice of French wine law, which seems to revolve around the idea that you either have a piece of sacrosanct land or you haven't.

When it comes to the importance of the winemaker, it is only people like the refreshing Anthony Barton, proprietor of two châteaux bearing his surname, who would give you an argument. But then he is of good Irish stock. Not for him the anxious mutterings about proportions of different grape varieties: nor has he time for half-witted journalists who produce lots of drivel in their obscure tasting notes (such as 'smells like wet dog hair') or who speculate about how the vintage is going to turn out before the grapes are even picked; nor, especially nor, those Americans who earnestly enquire 'Who is your winemaker?' and make a twee academic issue out of what is, after all, just a damn good drink.

Of his damn good drinks with which I had the pleasure to become acquainted, Langoa-Barton 1984 (still in cask) packs a thumping concentration of fruit, and Léoville-Barton 1984 (ditto) appears seductively supple, with more class and finesse, and with not a whiff of dog hair, wet or dry. The 1980 Langoa-Barton is one of many that proves his point about careless vintage notes: if anybody tries to tell you that 1980 clarets are a write-off point them to a bottle of this.

It's all very well being casual about making good wine when you meekly or otherwise inherit a nice little bit of earth, but Mr Barton's good friend down in the Graves, Peter Vinding-Diers, is not blessed with a century or more of tradition on which to park his Danish, jean-clad frame. He is the personification of the ultra new approach, bristling with science, much of it picked up in

Australia. He always stops to ask himself why things are done the way they are, and is the sort of man who wouldn't even take a bath without thinking of half a dozen alternative, logical, and more efficient ways of cleaning himself up.

Pick grapes and just press them? How barbaric, old chap! At Château Rahoul and Domaine La Grave he stacks the white ones in boxes overnight in order to get a bigger 'juice return'; more fruit flavour is brought about by enzyme activity in the grapes which begins only after picking; and by the following morning they are cool and ready for pressing, a circumstance which allows the 'varietal characteristics' to show themselves to greatest effect in the finished wine.

Then, oh you haven't heard the half of it, since it is yeasts on the grape skins which are responsible for the fermentation, he has isolated five different strains to be found in his vineyards, selected the best and had a supply dry-frozen by the Botanical Department at the University (in exchange for a case of wine). These are added to the must which is then fermented at 14°C in – get this – oak barrels.

Any resemblance to traditional practices at Château Mouton-Rothschild, the Bartons, or anywhere else is purely coincidental, since the philosophy is totally different. Take the revered soil, for instance. 'What soil?' asks Peter Vinding-Diers. 'The only influence of the soil is its moisture-holding capacity, nothing else.' But what about the minerals that vines are supposed to extract from dozens of feet underground, and which make Mouton's wine different from its neighbour Lafite's? 'If you examine them, you find that the trace minerals in grapes are not related to those in the soil,' says Peter simply.

He is not agitating for first growth honours, just making his own style of wine: fresh, flavoursome, full of taste and zip that is characterful yet affordable, and that can be relished without waiting for complicated things to happen to it over the course of a decade or more.

Inside every bottle of wine is a bit of the person who made it.

C'est tout.

'Rosie thinks I've nipped out for a pint!'

Honeysett

Claret Begins at Home

'Hmmm, something on the lines of a
"Mouton-Rothschild Premier Cru", you say.'

'If there's one thing I can't stand, it's wine snobbery.'

'Well, at least we won't have to buy any
vinegar for a few years.'

'Sow the grape pips in a rich soil against
a sunny wall ...'

'What would you like, Mavis – "Boots Station Road" or
"Boots Plaza Shopping Centre"?'

'I'll have a non-alcoholic beer and a fun-free salad.'

'Of course, Margaret working is a great help. She buys all her own gin.'

'*Cocktail parties, cocktail parties.*'

Stanley Reynolds

A SOBER PROPOSAL

Since becoming a literary editor, I have found that young persons are constantly coming up to me in the street, gripping me by the lapels, breathing in my face and asking: 'How do I become a top-notch writer?'

The answer I give them is simple. It is the same answer I always give. What you must do is drink. No one can possibly become a top-flight writer unless he drinks. I know this because I have seen it in the movies. But even before then I knew it in my bones; hence my own years of excessive drinking. But I, apparently, did not drink enough and that is why I am only a literary editor and not a first-rate author, staggering into my office and breaking my furniture.

Now I have further evidence in a new anthology of literary binges called *Those Drinking Days: Myself and Other Writers*: Ernest Hemingway, F. Scott Fitzgerald, Robert Lowell, William Faulkner, Malcolm Lowry, Thomas Wolfe, John O'Hara, Eugene O'Neill, Jack London, James Joyce, Jack Kerouac, Tennessee Williams, John Berryman, Theodore Roethke, and, well, just about everybody else including Samuel Beckett and the author of this book, a Mr Donald Newlove, who had to wait until he was forty before he got a novel published because he had dedicated himself to his art with such intensity that he often could not find the typewriter. In fact, sometimes he could not find the table and the chair. Indeed on some occasions he could not find the house or the street. And several times he could not find himself.

'That,' I tell young persons and women's clubs when I am called on to be a guest speaker, 'is just the ticket. Just the sort of dedication that a fellow needs to become a world-class author. If a young person lacks this dedication he will not make the grade. He will probably end up only teaching drinking at some poly or one of those cow colleges over in Yankland.'

I tell them, these women's clubs and young persons when they ask me, I tell them: 'Don't believe a word of it.' That's what I tell them. Sure I do. 'Drinking never hurt no authors,' I say. Look at Sinclair Lewis. Nobel Prize-winner. Ditto Ernest Hemingway. And same again Sam Beckett, know what I mean? All Nobel Prizes for literature. Sinclair Lewis had such dedication to his craft that you couldn't bring him anywhere without him busting up the furniture and once he got kicked out of some New York speakeasy and he sat down on the kerb with his feet in the gutter and said, 'What's the point of winning the Nobel Prize for Literature when you can't even get into a speakeasy?'

There is much talk about literary feuds and the general bitchiness of the trade but less is known about the real love and devotion that writers have for one another. Like James Joyce getting into arguments in low bars in Paris and then leaping behind Ernest Hemingway shouting, 'Deal wid 'em, Hemingway,' or the wonderful story of the established writer, Sinclair Lewis, giving a young man a hand-up and then the younger writer, in this case Thomas Wolfe who was six foot six and weighed nearly twenty stone, paying back this love and affection by beating the crap out of all Sinclair Lewis's enemies, which means anyone Lewis suddenly took a dislike to.

If, in this lecture, I appear to be ignoring Britain and concentrating on the United States and Ireland it is because America has dominated literature in this century. No doubt this is because when you go into a bar in America and order a whisky you get the equivalent of what would be a triple over here – where they hardly wet the bottom of the glass for you and they're always shutting the goddam pubs – plus the booze here is too low proof on account of they export all the high octane stuff to America and then of course in Britain we really do not possess any real rotgut like Old Tennis Shoes or some of that other Nobel jungle juice of America and then naturally, what with the goddam taxes over here we cannot really afford to buy imported stuff like that colossus of knockout drops, Stolichnaya vodka. It is little wonder that novelists have suffered in Britain this century.

But we must not forget Malcolm Lowry, ace British novelist and heroic drunk; a superman. Falling into the hands of the Philistines, poor Lowry was forced to undergo aversion therapy. This was a hideous torture in which he was given all the alcohol he wanted but added to it was something which made him sick. The idea was to put him off the stuff. Ladies and gentlemen, fat chance. Have I told you this story before? No? Okay, well, the average man can take about five days of this aversion thingy. Malcolm Lowry took ... are you sure I haven't told you this one before ? ... Anyway, he took 21 days of it and then ... Ha, ha, ha ... broke out of the place and went to a pub and drank non-stop for 48 hours. Inspiration. That's what he said. Drink was his inspiration, Lowry said. He always said that. In fact he'd hardly say anything else, sitting in the goddam corner going on and on about it until you wanted to scream. Jesus! I mean some of those drunks get so boring. Of course I know it all helps with their writing, but the way they go on and on saying the same thing I mean it's very boring that and also very repetitive.

Which leads me on, quite naturally, to my next point which is the myth that drunks are boring people who keep repeating themelves. This is simply not true. There is this new book which has just come out which is all about these writers like Ernest Hemingway, Scott Fitzgerald, Robert Lowell, William Faulkner, Malcolm Lowry, Thomas Wolfe, James Joyce, Jack London, Tennessee Williams, did I say Malcolm Lowry? Malcolm Lowry, Hart Crane, Samuel Beckett, in fact all the best writers of English who all drank a hellofa lot and it never hurt them, much. John Berryman jumped off a bridge, thinking he'd drown, ... ha ha ha ... except it was frozen solid, and what about Hart Crane, jumped off the back of a ship right into a shark's mouth. Some suicide that. Did I mention Raymond Chandler, trying to shoot himself with a pistol in the shower only he was so pissed he kept missing and the bullets kept flying through the walls into the next-door neighbour's flat? Elevated 'tec stories to a fine art, Raymond Chandler. Gave him inspiration. Lowry always said that. Absolutely swore by it. I mean he really believed it did, the booze, give him inspiration. And look at Joyce. You think anyone could write *Finnegans Wake* without the special inspiration of booze? I mean, you ever try to read that sober? And even the younger writers know booze is much better than pot for it. Inspiration.

Do not Seek,
> *and Eliminate nothing,*
> *concluded the Chinese*
> *Master of 840 B.C.*
Buddhism is a big bomb on the head
> *and it hurts*

You think Jack Kerouac could have written that if he hadn't been drinking?

Say, have you heard about this new book, Ernest Hemingway, Scott Lowry, no, Malcolm I mean .. yes, well, know what I mean?

January 1982

'Eenie, meenie, miney, mo – it's your round.'

Heath

TINY TOTS

Drink is an increasing problem amongst schoolchildren.

The Times

'Not for me –
I'm skipping.'

'Okay, okay, my mother doesn't need an operation, but she sure could use a drink.'

Fay Maschler

HARD CHEESE

If you go to Tesco's or Sainsbury's, or for that matter to Harrods or Paxton and Whitfield's, and pick up a piece of cheddar cheese labelled Farmhouse, it actually is made on a farm. I saw it being done yesterday at West Pennard in Somerset. Before the first world war there were at least three thousand farms making their own cheeses. Now there are about thirty but they are currently receiving every encouragement, incuding quotas, guarantees, centralised storage, grading and wholesaling, from the Milk Marketing Board. The four English cheeses that the Board guarantees come from farms not factories (when labelled with the words Farmhouse English Cheese inscribed in the black and orange symbol showing one cheese stacked on top of two other cheeses inside a circle) are Cheddar, Cheshire, Blue Cheshire and Lancashire.

I must admit I had always carefully avoided Farmhouse cheeses in the belief that anything called Farmhouse must come from a particularly depressing, clinical factory with an advertising programme heavy on pictures of waving wheat, dewy mornings, gnarled old field hands and tools that haven't been in use for the last hundred years. At Newton Farm in West Pennard the farmer Green had a suitable West Country burr but it wasn't milk maids and wooden pails and cheese cultures scraped off mucky boots, more like stainless steel pasteurising machines and large capacity storage vats and a gadget that cuts the curds and a culture delivered from the laboratories. However, the cheeses are not manufactured according to a rigid formula or computerised process as happens in a factory. The farmer monitors each tub of about two and a half thousand gallons of milk (taken from his own or neighbouring Friesian cows) and decides for how long it should be exposed to the culture, when the rennet should be added, for what time it should be cooked and at what point the curds should be cheddared, cut into blocks and stacked one on top of another and left to drain and solidify before salt is mixed in and the substance packed into molds and pressed into the cylindrical shapes we associate with real cheddar cheese.

It is not an infallible process. The day we visited, the culture (a new one) had not behaved as anticipated and the curds were sulkily sitting around letting it all hang out when they should have been knitting into dense thicknesses with the properties of elastic. Where once this would have represented a panicking loss of revenue to the cheese maker, these duff cheddars were going to be sold off thanks to the Milk Marketing Board to processors or some other users who view cheese as visible blocks of protein rather than a commodity with the class and sensitivities of, say, wine.

The successful cheddars, which is most of

them I gather, are carefully washed, wrapped in larded muslin, left to mature a month or two at the farm and then sent to the cheese store where they are graded and looked after, turned regularly, kept at the right coolness and humidity for anything from five to nine months until deemed ripe and interesting and then sold to businesses large and small, prestigious and plebeian. Speaking of the latter, it came as a shock to me that these real farmhouse cheeses are also parcelled up in vacuum packs and sold under the brand names of Black Diamond, St Ivel and Dairy Crest. To prove how image-conscious we all are, how we prefer the idea of the gnarled field hand to the conveyor belt monitor, the manager of the cheese store conducted a blind tasting of the block farmhouse cheddar and that from the cylinder with the rind. Of course they were cut in such a way that we couldn't see which was which and to a journalist (for it was a press outing I was on) we got it wrong, coming out strongly in favour of what we thought was the genuine olde worlde grocery shop cheese cut, likely as not, by a diminutive old man wielding a cheese wire, but which was, in truth, the block stuff.

'Don't touch the Stilton,' I said. 'It'll only trigger off your migraine.'

It is encouraging that demand for individually made cheese is on the increase. What with real ale, and real cheese, and real bread we may soon have real people again. I, for one, will strongly support the Campaign for Real People. Such citizens might well go further in their search for proper English cheese, a few of which are still being made in small quantities, not enough to interest the Milk Marketing Board, but worth searching out if you are in the appropriate area.

There is one farm that still makes Double Gloucester in Gloucester. It is at Dymock. The full cream milk comes from Gloucester cattle, of which only some 90 are left in the world. That cheese should be eaten reflectively. Cotherstone is a cheese with an open texture and a soft crust. It can be bought at Cotherstone Post Office and at Barnard Castle. The season ends with the first frost of autumn. Swaledale is a softish mild cheese made in a few farms around Grunton, North Yorkshire. Eskdale, something like a Camembert, is made from Jersey milk in the Cleveland district of Yorkshire. Sage Lancashire is made by a Mr and Mrs Butler who also provide Farmhouse Lancashire cheese. Flavoured with fresh or dried sage, it is available occasionally in Preston and some specialist cheese shops in other parts of the country.

Goat cheese never seems to have made much of a mark in England but there is one rolled in poppy seeds, paprika, mixed herbs and sesame seeds which you can get from Manor House Farm, Micklefield, near Leeds. It is sad to relate that no Farmhouse Stilton is made these days. It all comes from factories and the natural mold that once invaded from the outside has been synthesised and powdered and is now mixed into the curds thus reversing the natural way and causing the blueness to be thickest in the centre and least evident at the perimeter; an untrue state of affairs.

English regional cheese lovers often talk conspiratorially of hunting down real Dorset Blue Vinney. This was a cheese made from hand-skimmed milk, so the whey had a higher fat content than usual. Veining was helped along by a stir from an old horse brass. Word has it that the real thing no longer exists. Much alleged Blue Vinney is in fact reject Stilton. If you are interested in Farmhouse cheese, some farms in Cheshire and Somerset welcome visitors.

'Get back to the kitchen! When and if there
are any compliments you'll be notified.'

CONCLUSIVE
SCENE—*Hibernian Table d'hôte.*

'I want a hundred and twenty-eight get-well cards.'

Libby Purves

FEEDING-TIME BLUES

It is nine o'clock, and this is a hieroglyph on the back of my notepad to say *Sauce Cressonnière all over Sound Man's Back.* I want to remember it, I want to know it is not a bad dream, so I write it down. In case I forget it, same way as I forgot the bloody bloody spoon for hoity Mrs Corner-table's bloody bloody custard (all right, *Sauce Anglaise*), so I had to go back through the kitchen to find a spoon, and made Chef drop a ladleful of *Gratinée Normande* on his foot. Then after that, all the spoons were soupy, I had to wash up, and when I came out I had this inexplicable plate of salmon in my other hand and banged into the Sound Man, hence fragments of buttered watercress now congealing firmly to his M & S cashmere back. It all happened quite logically. Must cling to that: all perfectly logical. Not a bad dream.

The miserable bastards on centre table are baying for their main course, I suppose. What consideration can you expect from punters who order omelette at a time like this? How can I break it to Chef that they want two salmon, one lamb, one *omelette soufflé aux épinards*, the whole order involving five pans, in two of which he is currently trying to make *sauce anglaise* if the eggs would only stop curdling where the sweat drips on them?

When I say Chef, of course, I mean Husband. That is why I am here in the first place, for beneath that important puffed white hat dangles a mere amateur, a victim of the broadcasting process, doomed to make a public display of himself to provide bread

and circuses for the licence-payer. Well, circuses, I doubt whether he could make bread, right now, though there are a few tasty-looking stray croûtons stuck to the back of his trousers, he must have sat in them.

But I must not ramble. Collect thoughts. (Collect *noisettes d'agneau*, too, for demanding beak-nosed lady near the door, there you are madam, may I help you to some vegetables? With two forks, yes, we have a problem with the spoons.) To begin at the beginning: my husband, Heiney by name, is making a film for his *In At The Deep End* series on BBC1. He has moved on from sheepdog-training and Caine-throttling to become a Master Chef. His training is now well advanced: already he cannot steam a carrot without needing total silence in the kitchen, a clean white jacket, and a huge black attaché-case full of assassin's knives. After a lifetime of decent cooking, he has learned how to ruin perfectly good broccoli and carrots by mushing them up with double cream and stinking gelatine into a flabby terrine which lies in a pool of tomato vinaigrette like something Miss Marple might find on a library floor. With the Big Chefs competition not for another month, it has been decreed that he should first try out his skills in a realistic battleground. So trainee Chef, with his lady wife as background prop and waitress, must run a real restaurant for one evening.

It is, after all, one of the great ambitions of every middle-class Elizabeth David junkie: to throw it all in and run a super little bistro, with one partner knocking out *Koulibiaka* and cucumber sorbets while the other flits smilingly between the tables, making people happy. It is an innocent dream, and the chief reason why the average life of a restaurant in the UK is precisely two years. So we are to take one over for an evening, the two of us plus a friend as waitress, and feed twenty-eight hungry punters including – if he turns up – a Famous Chef.

And the film camera will creep between the tables, recording successes and failures and bits left on the side of the plates.

Unaccountably, nobody seems to have leapt forward with an offer to hand over Le Gavroche or Tante Claire to our management for the night. So we found ourselves at five o'clock in this obscure but established little joint in outer London, looking around the tiny premises (old church pews, tables apparently cobbled out of coffin-lids, misshapen pottery on shelves) with a dawning realisation that not only would the camera and sound men have trouble edging between the tables, but so would the serving staff.

Fortunately, the other waitress, Caroline, is narrower of hip than I; but even she foresaw a hard and bitter struggle to get the veg du jour between the customers' solid backs to feed the uttermost edges of the room. It is a bit like running an egg-and-spoon race through an overcrowded cowshed.

Around six, with four kilos of mange-tout lying smugly prepared in plastic colanders (severe dish shortage, PA's were running up and down the High Street outside looking for a Woolworth's at 5.25), we were getting quite bullish. Even the ten-by-three foot floor space in the kitchen seemed vaguely amusing, and squeezing past Chef's bum to get from cup-shelf to coffee-machine more quaint than disastrous. Nothing to it, this restaurant business. All you need is a bit of style and a charismatic chef who will fry salmon all evening, then come out and sit with favoured customers drinking brandy and roaring with Rabelaisian laughter till 3 a.m. Perhaps, we all said, laying out serving-cloths carefully on the nearest pew, we could get a few like-minded friends together and run a restaurant of our own in the disused Post Office down the road. Piece of cake. Chance to show off real home cooking, use fresh local produce. Lovely. We trotted downstairs to change into fresh-looking striped aprons, found the larger lavatory firmly locked up and discovered another, somewhat cramped, facility situated on a corridor reachable only by way of the narrow kitchen.

If it crossed our minds that customers, too, might require to pass this way, we suppressed the thought. Three of the film crew squeezed by as I bent to stack up boxes of coffee-filters, and I picked myself up laughing heartily, and went back to sculpting pretty patterns on the butter. Morale was high.

First customers at eight. Good evening, table for four, was it? May I take your coat, open your wine, light your candle? Very professional. After all, for two long school-holiday summers I was a real waitress, at a God-fearing family hotel in Ireland. I remember being made to change into a skirt that touched the knee, my 1960s mini being, in Mary the Cook's opinion, 'All very fine and good in the bar, but not in the doining-room.' I had a yellow nylon overall, and was by common consensus the worst waitress in West Cork; people used to turn up their collars and cower when I attempted silver service of the scampi, and I twice took out plates of Egg Mayonnaise with all the bits of curly radish and tomato roses on, but neither egg nor mayonnaise. The other chief memory, until this evening, was of Tony from Kerry, the washer-up, who took delight in turning the temperature of his machine up so high that the cutlery came out red-hot, and we had to toss it up and down like jugglers as we ran with burning fingers to re-lay the tables for the second wave of eaters. I now also remember the physical fatigue: the way we girls would sit silently around in the tiny store-room where we ate our meals, flexing swollen nyloned feet and staring vacantly up at the teetering piles of Erin freeze-dried vegetables stacked overhead.

The girls who run the restaurant most nights have multiple-choice menus like

GCSE papers, but we have opted for a simple, nay, stark choice. They can have vegetable terrine or onion soup, then they can have *noisette d'agneau* or salmon or – if they really must – omelette. Then they can have pudding and coffee, and push off home. We have failed to crack the cutlery storage system, so soup-spoons have to be recycled for pudding. We have only brought two vegetable dishes, and we forgot both serving- and stirring-spoons when we loaded the car up a hundred and forty miles away this morning. Well, not *forgot* exactly, not with the six Master Lists to consult, but the garage couldn't get the new fuel filter from Ipswich in time, so we took the other car at the last minute, and now as Chef cooks *sauce cressonnière* in London, his wooden spoon is four feet up on a hydraulic platform in Suffolk. This is not the most convenient *mise en place* for a highly trained Master Chef. It has intensified the spoon shortage. It occurs to me, in a rare lucid moment, that Mosimann and Roux probably do not have to put up with waitresses snatching spoons from Chef's very fingers to rinse off and put in front of pudding-eaters.

But none of this awkwardness need have led to the microphone chap colliding with the watercress sauce, nor indeed to the fact that we are all skating on spilt custard; that is, three of us, two of the film crew, a director, and a nice lady on her way to the washroom. No. The main obstacle to running a calm and orderly restaurant, the main source of chaos, is the customers.

One thing I had forgotten, from Irish days, was how very much waiters and waitresses get to hate the punters. There are too many of them. They sit awkwardly, so you can't get past. They make terrible, drunken, unfunny jokes when you are trying to give them peas. They eat too fast, and their empty plates stare reproachfully up at you when for the fourth time you stumble by with someone else's dinner, trying hard to obey Chef's hysterical instruction not to let the plate get cool because the sauce will separate. Customers are hell. They get in the way. They bring out the Basil Fawlty in me.

The only one I like is the Famous Chef, who has turned up at last, Gallic and beaming and affable. I fawn horribly upon him from soup to strawberry-studded pudding; but moments later and mere feet away, loathing of the customers boils up again. The Woman Who Sent Back The Salmon is complaining that her candle isn't lit. 'There you are,' I snarl, flourishing a match. 'Anything else that looks a bit pink, you just cook it yourself over that.' The next table is staring bitterly at his strawberryless pudding. 'Excuse me, miss, this isn't the same dessert I saw you taking to Monsieur Roux', he whines. I draw myself up to my full height, and then beyond that, to Basil Fawlty's height. 'Of course it isn't the same as he had! He's *French*, inny?'

It is a brief triumph. It will not get the washing-up done.

July 1986

'Police inspector, Sanitary inspector, Weights and Measures, Public Health, Fire Prevention, AA or RAC – whatever kind of inspector he is, we're in trouble.'

'Chicken nouvelle cuisine is the same as roast chicken but we get a graphic designer to lay out the veg.'

'Must be a Michelin inspector.'

'Knowing the service in this place, he could have been dead for days.'

'Inspector – there's the little matter of the cover charge.'

*'Don't you sometimes wish we could just queue for
our food, like other regiments?'*

'I refuse to divulge anything other than my name, rank and recipes!'

Clement Freud

PEAS IN OUR TIME

Peas are the most popular vegetable in the world. The average child will not eat beans, hates spinach, can't stand cabbage, won't give sprouts house-room but says, 'Oh good, peas.'

Adults by and large accept peas; they are considered the safe vegetable at banquets and it is very sad that we as a nation now seem to be too busy to buy them in the pod and shell them. What comes out of packets of frozen peas is reasonably all right – though there is none of the crispness that comes from the fresh vegetable. What emerges from tins of English peas is depressing, with few exceptions: unlike French and Belgian tins and cans which are better.

The French also produce *petits pois à la française*, which are peas stewed with onion and lettuce and carrot, and a great treat.

Now is the time to buy fresh peas; the shops are full of them, and one of the great points in their favour is that it takes no great skill to determine which are fresh and which old. If it is tender beef that you require, you need a modicum of expertise. Should you set your sights on a ripe melon, the only way to identify one ready for the table is by squeezing and smelling – which requires courage, especially if the fruiterer is bigger than you are. But peas are easy.

If they have been picked recently, which is what you should have in mind, they are pale green and soft and have a slight sheen; the rest are yellowish, dull of hue and hard. The best pods are those which clearly contain peas a-plenty waiting to jump out, and these are also the most economical buy; it takes as long to open a pod containing one pea as it does to unzip one holding seven. If you buy well, the progeny of a pound of pods is about enough for three people.

There is really only one satisfactory way to boil peas: you put them in the minimum amount of boiling water required to cover what you have, seasoning the water with salt and sugar (sugar makes the water boil more hotly) and after three to six minutes, depending on the size of the peas, you drain them and put them back into the pan with butter. Cover the pan, simmer for another minute or two and strew with sugar, if you like sugar, and salt.

One of the great English dishes is a pea omelette. A spoonful of fresh small garden peas, cooked as above, simmered in half an ounce of butter, all of which (butter and peas) are then incorporated into two well-beaten large eggs and made into an individual omelette. If the art of omelette-making has escaped you (you need a heavy pan which should be tremendously hot so that you can cook and mix the omelette in the air rather than on the stove) then you can make a similarly delicious dish by scrambling them: the same mixture, add a spoonful of cream and cook over a very cool flame in a pan brushed generously with butter, stirring lazily with a wooden spoon as the bottom of the mixture sets.

In China they spit; even those who love China tend to be slightly disenchanted by the rich retching that takes place in public, and quite often private, places. They do peas in the pod, nicely boiled in salted water and you put the pod in your mouth, suck out the peas, munch on the pod and spit out what remains. As this is exactly what we do at jellied eel stalls, I do not know why we don't try Chinese peas from the same barrow.

If peas get older, as they do, a quite delicious way of serving them is to cook them with herbs – mint, basil, tarragon, even dill accompaniment to starters like salami and ham and pâté and melon.

And so to mushy peas – without which no north country pie or fish shop could hold up its head. These are usually made with dried peas, but the sort of peas about which I warned you at the beginning of the page – what comes from old and hard and discoloured pods – will do nicely. You stew them in water and grated onion and salt and a touch of Marmite, though none of the last three ingredients seem to be very important. The essential thing is to cook them for a long time; there is absolutely no kudos in underdone mushy peas.

June 1982

'Bleedin' Trades Description Act!'

or fennel leaves – and, after draining and buttering, warm them in butter and anoint them with boiled double cream.

Pea soup is lovely and iced pea soup has much to recommend it. You take the water in which you have boiled the peas and cook the pods in this until they are tender – about fifteen minutes. Add a soup-cube, put into a blender or food-processor, then pass through a sieve and thicken with cream; you serve this hot with cubes of bread fried in bacon fat, or iced, with an extra swirl of cream and rock salt and chives.

In Italy they serve peas with rice and a very happy mixture this is. I have had it hot: nicely boiled rice blended with properly boiled peas, garnished with Parmesan cheese to make the mixture tacky and strewn with extra grated cheese which can, but need not be, browned under a grill.

The same mixture, rice and peas, incorporated in a mayonnaise is also a good

Peter McArthur

FOR BRITISH CONSUMPTION

DEAR MR PUNCH,—This morning I was strolling in the Strand, meditating on the sad fact that I am now three thousand miles from Broadway and can't swim, when I suddenly found myself in front of the American Quick Lunch Restaurant.

Says I to myself, 'Here's where I get glad. I shall go get a piece of pie like mother used to make, and listen while the girls use language to the chef.'

The outside of the place looked all right, with the chef browning the sinkers in full view of an admiring crowd, but the first step inside gave me a jolt. This was no Nassau Street quick lunch, but a cross between Delmonico's and Dennett's,★ that had suffered 'a sea change into something rich and strange.'

Thinking it might improve on acquaintance, I took a seat in front of a palatial mirror and tried to imagine that I had just stepped around the corner off Park Row to wrassle some sustaining hash before going to do my afternoon stunt in the famine district of a yellow journal. (The famine district is familiarly known as the literary department.)

'Buckwheat cakes and a cup of black coffee,' I said to the waitress, and then perked up my ear expectantly.

'Thank you, Sir,' she said as politely as if she had never walked 'farther than Finsbury.'

What's the use of having an American Quick Lunch without the local colour? If I had given that order in a New York quick lunch bean emporium it would have been translated to the chef's department in this fashion:

'Three up and draw one on the dark!'

Think how that would have toned up the frayed system of an exile, and what an exhilarating fillip it would have given to a correct islander!

What does it matter to me that the pies, shortcakes, beans, and all American dishes are as advertised, if I can't have the language

HEATH

* Delmonico's – the most expensive restaurant in New York.

Dennett's – the regulation cheap restaurant – the original 'quick lunch.'

with it? When I order an omelette in a hurry I want to hear the waitress sing out:

'A slaughter in the pan, and no waiting.'

Poached eggs can never be the same to me unless they come as 'Whitewings, sunny side up,' and I want my veal cutlet as 'A slab of a yearlin' for a gummer.' Pork and beans should come as 'Chicago and Boston', and a small coffee as 'One in a shell.'

Besides, they served me pie without cheese!

While the new Quick Lunch appears to be thoroughly convincing to the untravelled Englishman, it somehow lacks flavour to a homesick invader.

August 1903

'*Forget the Beverly Hills Diet. Don't even* **think** *about the Scarsdale method. Stick with the F-plan high-fibre, and drink lots of orange juice.*'

Alan Whicker

A LAND FLOWING WITH YOGHURT AND CARROT JUICE

Anyone can be beautiful and loved: it's just a question of applying something, take a course, buying a pot, denying yourself – or being operated on, slightly. So say the Arch-priests of the religion of beauty, which women spend £100,000,000 a year to practise. To keep up in the Face Race, the average woman in her lifetime also spends four years fourteen weeks and six days in front of her mirror, making-up. It certainly feels that way when you're waiting downstairs.

Men – apart from the fringe fringe – seem unprepared to do much, though still pay-out a crafty £8,000,000 a year; would you believe – *guy*lashes!

By the end of this decade Americans will have spent £4,000,000,000 to make them-

'The thin man inside me keeps getting hungry.'

selves a little lovelier each day – or maybe, to buy a little hope. In view of all this I went to Texas (of course) to observe a species in The Greenhouse, that ultimate purpose-built fat farm which cost a million pounds to contrive and is quite improbable. It stands, a perfumed palace outside Arlington, bathed in the soft glow of money and dedicated to the sale of dreams, the expectation of beauty.

Women of a certain age (and some younger) queue to pay from £50 to £110 a *day* for rejuvenation. Some stay months. The ageing and wrinkled, the plump and bored surrender dollars and dignity in exchange for solace and repair, for the dream of growing younger, fairer, sexier … while outside in the harsh sunlight, gardeners symbolically dye dry Texas grass green.

In Britain where we at least let grass decide its own colour, narcissism is also in – observe the march of fully booked Health Farms. Prices may be less extreme but you can still lose, along with avoirdupois, some ninety guineas a week.

A Health Farm means paying a lot of money *not* to do something. At the end of the week you could get a breathtaking bill for what you could easily have done at home for nothing if you had the strength of character, which you haven't – so pay up and look small.

I was introduced to an early version fifteen years ago, surrendering to its rigours for a radio programme, and later for *Panorama*. Afterwards a number of patients, affronted by evident truths and being filmed Before instead of After, complained to the BBC. They did not notice I was hooked on the good sense of it all.

Such instant affront is one of the problems of television: nobody wants an accurate image of anything near to home; the preferred picture is blurred, gently distorted, romanticised, approving.

'Strawberry mousse! Strawberry mousse!'

I filmed a *Whicker's World* programme on a most enjoyable cruise. Afterwards the shipping line spokesman said ruefully: 'It was an honest programme, all right. The only trouble was, it was *too* honest.' That's the way it goes, tellywise.

At this Surrey health hydro a few were ill but the majority were, quite reasonably, carboholics resisting the temptation, alcoholics drying-out, executives escaping the telephone: 'My Chairman goes to the South of France and puts on a stone. I come here and lose one. He feels guilty; I feel great.'

Health farms vary from earnest nature cure centres catering for those with little faith in orthodox medicine to stately but antiseptic Victorian mansions where society matrons hold back the years and Show Biz straightens its elbow and resists the sweet smell of excess.

If you are *not* sick there's no doubt one of the cheerier hydros, fully of jolly folk expensively repenting excess, is more agreeable than those chintzy halls where arthritic old ladies knit by the fireside, each a silent reproach to the healthy but weak-willed who just want to lose a few pounds, regardless.

Voluntarily incarcerated in one of the serious establishments, I was watching a television play one night amid an enthralled group in dressing gowns; just getting to the exciting bit when a young man in the statutory white Kildare-coat strode in and switched the set off in mid-sentence. I leapt up in outrage.

'Ten o'clock,' he said, reproachfully. 'Time for bed.' I was about to dash him to the ground when it came to me this was what we were paying for: a return to the secure days of Nanny-knows-best.

Once you've accepted such discipline there's a certain relief in surrendering to white-coated father-figures who know what's good for you, in having your days planned down to the last orange juice. There's the grin-and-bear-it Dunkirk spirit of the carrot cocktail bar where you swop losses; the lazy pastoral pleasures of a country estate; the satisfaction of growing, if not a little lovelier, at least a little *smaller* each day.

I remember another Correspondent in Ismailia during the riotous days when the Egyptians put a match to Shepherds, the late Bernard Wicksteed who wrote Tubby Hubby columns for the *Daily Express*; when he left his first health farm, he told me, he was 'walking a foot off the ground.' There surely is new delight in old suits that not only fasten without strain, but hang loose.

We are today in the middle of an expansionist trend, with 10 million men and 12 million women overweight. Insurance companies say a man of 45 who is 25 pounds above his proper weight lowers his expectation of life by 20%. Put another way, he'll die at 60 when he might have reached 80 . . . We spend £25 million a year on slimming foods which taste like crushed cardboard, lotions, massage equipment, pills; but you lose it best by practising one simple exercise, performed sitting down – and don't think it's easy. You shake the head from side to side when offered a fattening plateful.

A sensible girl I took out in New York refused her apple pie à la mode with the telling comment: 'A moment on the lips, a lifetime on the hips.'

Americans, needless to say, have the ultimate diet: the Zero-Calorie, which means you just don't eat. As you might expect, it works.

Elaine Johnson, a 35-year-old housewife,

was almost 20 stone and so fat she couldn't cross her legs, or sit without breaking the chair. She started the diet after getting wedged in a cafeteria doorway, a significant time to face facts. In four months she lost eight stone. At the same California hospital Bert Goldner weighed 425 lbs – almost 4 cwt – and was so spherical he couldn't sit or lie without fainting from lack of oxygen. He had to sleep standing up or kneeling. During a nap he once toppled over and broke his leg.

You see how helpful it is – *reading* about diets. I feel thinner already.

The form at a fat farm is a Sunday arrival with a pseudo-medical test that evening: blood pressure, heart beats, weight and the old Army how-do-you-feel routine. The usual treatment is a complete fast, by which they mean three oranges a day. Should you be determined to surrender the whole hog, three glasses of water each day, with a slice of lemon to take the taste away.

Mornings are filled with mild action: osteopathy, ultra-sonic therapy, infra-red and radiant heat, saunas, steam and sitz baths, various combinations of sweat-inducing bakery: mud, wax, cabinet, peat, blanket baths.

Best of all, massage and manipulation which comes in all possible forms, from pleasurably painful to Wake up, Sir. As I always say, it's nice to be kneaded; but a health farm's asexual: all slap, no tickle.

Looming ominously behind such agreeable time-fillers: enemas and colonic irrigations. Nature cure enthusiasts explain that in decoking the engine, waste poisons must be swept away for a fresh, empty start – and that's the way they gotta go. This may be medically sound but true or false, it's not much fun.

Various spin-off activities, or non-activities, seem more therapeutic: complete rest (or stultifying boredom); non-availability of demoralising distractions, like pleasure; the

BANX

'Some days I wish we could go to a fish restaurant.'

spiritually up-lifting sensation of being above temptation, per force.

I derived additional benefit by giving up smoking 50 a day, on the assumption that if I had to be unhappy anyway, I might as well be utterly miserable. On a fast, mouth coated with dark fur, cigarettes are resistible and the whole system so outraged that one further deprivation goes unnoticed. I commend this ploy to the addicted.

I also – giant stride for one man – cleaned my car. This beneficial, constructive exercise can occupy an afternoon or two. Unfortunately I have had no time for health farms during the past five years, so the car now needs another visit even more than I do.

The Metropole at Brighton recently opened the largest health hydro in Europe. I attended its inaugural week-end; a cheery group drinking mimosas on a private pullman train, inaugural lunch, a week-end of fun and slimming treatment. Without any effort, I put on five pounds.

This hydro may now close, the management realising what anyone as weak-willed as I could have told them before we left Victoria: serious dieting demands mon-

astic seclusion – several thousand acres and long country lanes between you and the nearest steak house. At the Metropole the Other World was down there in the dining-room every night, visibly stuffing, while outside on the promenade, the ice cream bars beckoned . . .

Nature cure is not merely an expensive folly; ignoring its unworldly cancer-cure fringe, the theory seems eminently reasonable: rest, restraint, simple food. The advantage of a farm's outrageous expense is that one may be stunned, upon release, into sensible eating. Write off those who triumphantly smuggle crummy tuck into bedrooms, or creep off on afternoon dainty-crawls; their weight problems are here to stay.

The ideal fortnight, down on the farm, is ten days' fast (during which you lose a stone), and four days' gentle return, via yoghurt, salads and plain food; this puts four pounds back into that shrunken stomach. The more flab you take, the more you leave behind; heavy drinkers and the very fat see it drop away, revealing long-lost toes.

Mealtime behaviour after release depends

upon your good sense and the impact of the bill. Most edge slowly back to the weight they took with them; sterner souls change their life pattern, better and smaller people for ever.

All right – so I got the car cleaned.

March 1971

Jack Trevor Story

COLD MEAT

As a dark and handsome young man with Brylcreemed hair and pointed patent-leather shoes, waiting to become a dance-band leader, I was lucky enough to work in cold meats. The manager of the shop asked me what I wanted to be and I told him frankly that I wanted to be dance-band leader. I did not want him to think that cold meats were the limit of my ambition.

'This is the very place to start then,' he said. 'We can teach you your counterpoint.' When I asked him what I had to do – his name was Marlow – he said that I had to wear a white coat and apron and when customers came in I was to point at the counter.

'Haslet, saveloy, chitterlings, tripe, breakfast sausage, Black Pudding, poloni, ham, York ham, corned beef, pressed beef, roast beef, roast pork, jellied veal, tongue, potted meat, faggots, veal-ham-and-egg pie, pork pie, sausage rolls, steak-and-kidney pies, milk cheese, cream cheese, red cheese and white cheese, St Ivel, treacle tart, don't forget the bacon –'

He then sucked in a great Norman Wisdom mouth-organ note and continued, 'Streaky bacon, back bacon, collar bacon, flank bacon, gammon bacon, shoulder bacon, forehocks and hocks. Green bacon, smoked bacon, Danish bacon, English bacon, rabbits, chickens and three kinds of dripping. Who's your favourite band-leader?'

'Roy Fox.'

'What's your instrument?'

'Guitar.'

'Well, take your geetar and geetartovere!'

You've guessed it; I had fallen amongst a comedian.

On Thursday afternoons he had two painted women down in the brine cellar on sacks of sawdust. I had to go out for cream buns and take care of the counter trade. Thursday afternoon is early closing except in the cold meat business. Monday afternoon was early closing for Marlow but work in the slaughterhouse for me. The animals were electrocuted, stabbed, shot and bled; I had only dance-band sort of jobs but they included balancing two buckets of blood on my carrier bike all the way back to the factory for the puddings.

Workhouses were rather more obvious then than now – these days they are euphemistic with social workers; the tramps sit around hand-out offices but then they were more colourful and shuffled into our shop as they left town for the ditches. Marlow prepared what he called lucky dips for them at a penny and tuppence each. These were surviving scraps of mildewed edibles – we had no refrigerators. Maggoty pieces actually *moving* with new life he saved for blind tramps.

Nothing was wasted. One of my continuing tasks was turning bits of fat into dripping; I had a big pork-dripping tin on a gas ring, all day long. The little cinders were carefully screwed into bits of greaseproof paper for tramps and undergrads – it was a twin-poverty trade in Cambridge.

'Don't give the gowns any mildew.' That was one of my instructions after somebody had got a report on a roast jowl of pork from

'Do you think the newts were off?'

'Rabbit, Sir?'

'You jump about and then they notice you and then they eat you.'

the Pathology lab. Gradually I got to know the grumblers – Alastair Cooke, Michael Redgrave, Hugh Foot, the Earl of Birkenhead, Arthur Marshall and Gilbert Harding and one or two blacks – Gandar-Dower. Selwyn Lloyd got some maggots and we had to give him a poloni free of charge. He ate it in the shop.

'If it stinks pour formalin on it. You're a dance-band leader, I shouldn't have to keep telling you.' Marlow again.

It became so that he was making fun of my style. Style has always been one of my things. Walking.

'Have you got a bad foot?' my daughter-in-law asked me yesterday. I limp to break the monotony. Without a dance-band at present, I conduct myself. Rubbing olive oil over mildewed bacon and black pudding or melting mouse-prints off dripping is not stylish. I had to cycle from the eggmart with six or seven score of eggs without breaking one. If I broke one I had to swallow eleven raw, otherwise it would be noticed.

Brawn I was good at. You can't get brawn now. I bought some recently and it was rubbish. The jelly was artificial. Jelly is the whole secret of brawn. Anyone can chop up a pig's head and sprinkle the whiskers in.

One day I got back to the shop and found Queen Mary sitting in Mr Marlow's accounts chair fanning herself with a butter pat. She used to come to Cambridge out of season to buy cheap antiques and she had seen a terrible accident at East Road Corner – or so she thought.

'There's a dead boy on Donkey's Common and the gutters are running with blood,' Mr Marlow told me, quietly.

'That's pigs' blood!' I cried. I had got knocked off my bike and into a bus and the Black Pudding buckets had gone flying. I was unconscious for ten minutes and then allowed to walk back to the shop.

'Don't go to a doctor,' Marlow said. He was afraid of getting the shop in trouble under the Act. I was taken home to Green End Road (107, still there) in the Royal Roller. For the record, I met Queen Mary once more when I took a banned turning (late Forties) at London University, not noticing the signs in Gower Street, and found my Austin Seven radiator halted by that formidable mobile throne. Though that's not, strictly speaking, shops. I am, however, on these occasions, cold meat.

June 1982

LARRY'S BUTCHERS

Miles Kington

BRING ON THE SUBSTITUTES

ALCOHOL

Now that a tobacco substitute has been devised, research is rushing ahead in other fields. Here's a progress report.

People drink for so many different reasons – to relax, to get maudlin, to have a good fight, to write a great novel – that more than one substitute is needed. Scientists have now isolated six different substances which will be marketed separately.

Lachrymosogens have the property of inducing a state of self-pity and instant recall of all grudges within ten minutes; in laboratory tests they can reduce nine out of ten rats to tears immediately, leaving the tenth rat staring hopelessly into the distance. But there is absolutely no damage to liver or kidneys. To be sold as Bitter Brew.

Machismogens leave the imbiber feeling that he could take on any man in the bar and beat him; when they are combined with vitamins, he probably could. A mustard-derived base gives a fiery taste to make up for the absence of alcohol. To be sold as Very Strong Old Pugilist.

Charismogens have the property of making the taker feel that given a typewriter and enough paper he could knock out a masterpiece before closing time, without actually falling over. Will be sold as Hemingway Special, Double Dylan and E. M. Forster's.

M60 is a chemical compound which marginally increases one's driving ability. Hop-, grape- or juniper-flavoured, it will be sold as One For The Road.

Hopwort is a simple country infusion, alcohol-free, for those addicted to the taste of real ale: rugby players, Guardian readers etc. Tastes potently of hops, barley, yeast, barrels, sawdust, etc. To be sold as Thakestons Amazing Old Froth.

Panaceamine is a newly discovered substance which, like alcohol, gives the taker the feeling that he could solve the world's problems if only he had the spare time, and the problems of those at the bar with him at any time. To be brewed by Jung's of Wandsworth.

SWEETS

The British addiction to sweets causes such widespread troubles as obesity, tooth decay, gum stuck under cinema seats and forgotten chocolate deposits in jacket pockets. For years scientists have been searching for a non-sweet lump without a wrapper which would slowly melt in the mouth but the nearest they have come so far is the ice lolly.

There are three prototypes still being researched.

1. A saliva-based cube which would gradually be reconstituted as spit.
2. A peppermint flavoured soya-based

object which, when rolled around the mouth and chewed, would clean the teeth.

3. A chewing gum which did not lose its flavour.

The basic drawback to all these is that they all either taste or feel awful, so work may switch to a small lump of chewy plastic which, when the flavour has gone, can take a cheap refill. On the other hand, it may be cheaper to devise a cinema seat to which gum will not adhere. On the other hand, this will not cure obesity. All in all, research is still at an early stage. Meanwhile sweet addicts are advised to stick to sweets which contain mostly air (mints with holes, aerated chocolate etc.).

PILLS

The best thing you can say about aspirins, sleeping pills, sedatives, pep pills and all the other little tablets we stuff ourselves with is that at least they are non-fattening. Scientists have already devised a substitute for pills: the placebo, a harmless chalky tablet which does the patient good because he thinks it is the real thing. But addiction to these is now on the increase and scientists are currently looking for a placebo substitute. The following are being developed.

1. A non-melting placebo, which can be spat out.

2. A soluble water-based pill which, when dissolved, leaves a glass of water behind.

3. An empty wrapper, the wrapper to be chewed.

4. Aniseed balls.

5. Gin and tonic.

6. A good book, lots of exercise and no mucking around.

HEALTH FOOD

Although health foods in moderation can do you a certain amount of good, research shows that a health-only diet can lead to serious effects – dangerously glowing cheeks, intestines scrubbed clean by roughage, unexercised stomachs, vitamin resistance and irritable restlessness caused by untapped energy. The ill-effects of health food fixation *can* be lessened by the sensible use of cream buns, sliced bread and lots of butter, but for those addicts who cannot bring themselves to eat non-health foods, the following aids are being developed.

1. Look-alike oatmeal, made from flaked white bread.

2. 'Organically grown' stickers, which can be placed on any normal food.

3. A new range of yoghurt in six flavours: Danish pastry, candy floss, marzipan, gin and tonic, valium and Old Holborn.

4. Soya substitute, tasting exactly like soya but reconstituted from best smoked bacon.

5. 'Normal' brown rice: in other words, real white rice stained with chocolate dye.

6. German Muesli: an appetising mix of chopped milk chocolate, pastry, biscuit, macaroon, marshmallow and Turkish delight, served with white sugar and condensed milk.

For details of research on these and other substitutes, e.g. for tea, coffee, potato crisps and sex, please write to the Ministry of Health Warnings, Whitehall, SWI.

July 1977

Fay Maschler

COOKS' TOURS

Elizabeth David wrote in her preface to *The Gentle Art of Cookery*, 'I wonder whether I would ever have learned to cook at all had I been given a routine Mrs Beeton to learn from instead of the romantic Mrs Leyel with her rather wild and imagination-catching recipes.' Like any first experience, the first cook book is obviously crucial to later development. A clumsy or unsympathetic first cook book can lead to a lifetime of indifferent and dreary cooking. A chance encounter in a book shop might later change everything but there have been cases where cooking has stopped altogether.

The range of cook books is such that the serendipity as described above is but a faint chance, which would explain why there are, on the whole, so few good cooks. I have been looking through a bibliography of cookery books published in 1975 – during the year it was compiled over 300 cookery books were published in Great Britain alone – and the list, which is by no means complete, adds up to over 1,700 books. Clearly almost anyone feels qualified to write a cookery book and there are surprising little tributaries in life that merit their own recipes.

Australian Cooking for the Diabetic and Overweight is one. Is it that fatties and diabetics crave novelty in their lives? Give us

'Guess what! We're now appearing in fish fingers – anonymously, of course'.

some Australian food they plead. But no. There is as yet no British or American publisher. It is a local book. Australian diabetics may seem a small sub-section in the international market but how many blacksmiths hard of hearing can be wanting to learn the gentle art? *The Deaf Smith Country Cookbook* has been published both here and in the United States of America (here only in paperback). Further investigation reveals that Deaf Smith was a celebrated figure in the Texas Revolution of 1835 and this is a health food book dealing in part with grain, and grain grows in Texas.

It seems convoluted reasoning but then cookery book authors are unstoppable when in search of a title. *Mary Bought a Little Lamb and This is How She Cooked It* sounds a particularly ghastly book with its overtones of slaughter of the innocent (it was, goodness knows, only following her to school). Is this the real explanation of 'and everywhere that Mary went the lamb was sure to go'? My rhetorical style develops from reading through the long list of titles, many of which are couched in the interrogatory vein.

What's Cooking on Okinawa? is a book you might feel better equipped to answer had you perused your *What's Cooking in Guyana and Carifesta '72 Cook book? The Something Went Wrong What Do I Do Now Cookery Book?* by John and Marina Bear has 200 pages of explanations which surely could be condensed into one or two tidy ideas like, start again, or, slide it carefully into the nearest dustbin. A work listed that I particularly liked for its bleak, hapless quality – it might have been written by Ibsen – is *What Have You Eaten in Norway?* Skirting the obvious ripostes like, not much, or, boiled cod, it suggests that it is about to reveal singularly unpleasant facts to rebound on your holiday or visit; a Norwegian joke.

In the spirit of untempting titles, and curiously cookery books specialise in these, mention must be made of *Plants Unsafe for Wine Making.* Though not a book you might rush to buy, it is an important trend to be acknowledged in the mania for publishing cook books. Having exhausted optimistic or positive subjects, authors could turn to such considerations as *100 Things You Can't Do with Celery,* or, *Understanding Why So Very Few People Like Sweetbreads.*

'*Apparently his carbonades flamandes is the talk of Dodge City.*'

With options like the above, it was indeed fortuitous that Mrs David first encountered Mrs Leyel and not, for example, Marian Fox and Lois Levine's *Come for Cocktails – Stay for Supper*, which would have been unlikely, I think, to have resulted in works of such culinary thrill and erudition as *Italian Food* or *Spices, Salts and Aromatics in the English Kitchen*. My first book was *The Radiation Cookbook*, a manual put out by the makers of Radiation gas stoves and I was pleased to hear from Len Deighton that it was his first cookbook too. Those terse recipes must have had more to them than an education in what is meant by Regulos 1–9, a unit of measurement as English and archaic sounding as bushels and pecks. Incidentally, Len Deighton grew up to write a book called *Où est Le Garlic?* revised and republished in 1979 as *Basic French Cooking* which is in my opinion one of the best primers to French Cookery, written with a keen sense of the relevant. As he says, he is providing the rules of the game. It is up to the reader how it is played.

Which brings us to the point that whatever book you begin with and however many you go on to accumulate, there comes a moment, or there should do, when you scarcely need cookery books at all. It is not an often publicised fact, but fact it is, that not all recipes are infallible or even accurate. You are not required to suspend judgement. If a dish you are cooking seems to you cooked, then it most probably is. There is no need to sit out the time stated by the cookbook. If the amount of sugar stated in the recipe seems to you a lot, then leave some out. The result will be that the dish is agreeably less sweet. These simple facts, and similar, seem to elude otherwise intelligent persons who cook as if a recipe were a prescription, with the result often more medicinal than delicious.

Though illustrated books are an aid to the inexperienced cook, before you strive to tease your dish into looking like the colour pic., let me warn you that the compilers of such books often called The Complete Book of... or 500 Recipes for... sometimes collate from their files the wrong photograph for the recipe. There are certain books well worth having, including your first inspiration, but it is the moment when you take the responsibility upon yourself for the recipe that your cooking will be serious.

'Then cook gently over a low heat until the grains are fluffy, without sticking together.'

Clement Freud

DREAMS OF IDEAL FOOD

My political colleagues would be shocked . . . but in an Ideal World there will be an almost unlimited number of hard-working, under-paid, obedient and faithful staff.

About eating then.

Breakfast consists of a bowl of stewed Cape Gooseberries and a glass of chilled juice extracted from pink Florida grapefruit. Then a pause before Grape Nuts served with soft brown sugar and Gold Top Milk . . . in fact, there will be no other colour seal upon milk bottles. On high days and holidays an Egg Benedictine – softly poached egg on grilled muffin garnished with Parma ham and decorated with a hollandaise sauce. For weekdays warm, crisp croissants, unsalted butter and ginger marmalade.

(The Ideal World will have done away with frozen food, dried herbs, taste stimulants and preservatives quite apart from desiccated coconut and Dr Scholl sandals which had no place even in the faultiest of civilisations.)

We move smoothly to elevenses, for tea or coffee were only compromises to sobriety and have little intrinsic merit.

A ripe peach, preferably a ripe white peach, skinned, liquidised, moistened with Armagnac and topped with a half bottle of Roederer's Crystal Brut Champagne should be served in a large Waterford glass (which you keep in a deep freeze, do you not?) and is almost bound to stave off actual hunger-pains until it is time for luncheon. Bake a few Pentland Javelin potatoes in a roasting tray covered with a layer of rock-salt; when

soft cut in halves, remove most, but not all, of the soft interiors and fill the resultant cavities with spoonsful of Beluga Caviar topped with a little soured cream and some hard-boiled egg yolk pressed through a sieve. You would be foolish to drink less than quite a lot of very cold Russian Vodka with this.

Grouse next; grouse is available at all times of the year, all birds being plump and female. Stuff the interior with well seasoned butter, drape a thin slice of hard pork fat over the breast and bake in a hot oven for 25 minutes before removing the fat and giving her a final 5 minute blast of heat.

The grouse is served on a slice of brioche fried in very hot sunflower oil until crisp and golden, then spread with the heart and liver of the bird simmered in butter, minced and spiked with crushed white peppercorns.

For accompaniment to the grouse, a gravy made by dissolving the juices of the roasting pan with burgundy; a bread sauce extravagant with cream and chopped onion, soft white crumbs and a touch of ground clove . . . and golden crumbs made by toasting a cut milk loaf under a warm grill until very dry . . . then crushing the slices with a rolling pin.

Pommes Soufflé are a pleasant accompaniment and in an ideal world they will not have to be made with the care and attention which is currently required in selecting the type of tuber, the thickness of the slice and the two temperatures of fat which cause the potato discs first to blister and then to puff.

The Salad is constructed of watercress and corn – what the French call *Marche* and the Germans *Rapunzel* – dressed with olive oil and rock salt and the grated rind of half a lemon. You stir until the salt is dissolved in the oil and mix with the greenery at the last moment, else the leaves will wilt. (The absence of acidity in the dressing is intended to make for greater enjoyment of the 1969 magnum of Remanee Conti.)

Complete the meal with a dish of wild

strawberries and a glass of Eau de Vie de Framboise from the deep freeze.

About sustenance to tide you over the afternoon void, before the arrival of the smoked swordfish canapes, the parmesan and cayenne puff pastry straws and the glass of Kir, made by adding 1978 domaine bottled Sancerre to a glug of Syrop de Cassis (no, Ribena will not do). On balance I am in favour of nothing at all, so that dinner can be properly appreciated (though there is a firm in Corsicana, Texas, that bakes an amazing cake so richly packed with cherries and almonds, pineapple and angelica that one is tempted to try a slice with the tea-time Pimms.)

Colchester Number One Oysters . . . with a little lemon juice.

Young green English Asparagus . . . with a soft mousseline sauce.

Suckling Pig, the skin scored and roasted to perfect crispness; the interior stuffed with truffled forcemeat.

New Potatoes simmered in cream and chopped chives.

Ratatouille of fresh tomatoes, sweet peppers, baby marrow, Spanish onions and aubergines baked in olive oil and white wine and fresh basil and green peppercorns and finally –

Chanterelles on toast.

The toast crisp and dry; the chanterelles, those most delectable of all edible fungi, well washed, carefully dried, before you give all those that are larger than the top joint of your little finger to the staff – and simmer the rest in a mixture of butter and bland oil until properly cooked.

Serve Poire William liqueur with the crystallised ginger; keep Grahams 1948 Vintage Port for the Farmhouse Blue Cheshire Cheese (Bath Oliver biscuits are best) and remember and be grateful that this is part of your calorie controlled diet.

What is more, in an ideal world, Alka Seltzer will be unnecessary and silent.

January 1980

'I don't care what your mother thinks, you just take it from me, kid, with ambrosia you don't need greens.'

'It's all new to them at the moment. Wait till they've been here a few years.'

'What wine goes with husky?'

Merrily Harpur

FLIES WITH EVERYTHING

'I know an amusing little place – very informal and low-key but bags of atmosphere ...'

*'This is nearly perfect; if **only** it could be on my expense account.'*

'A pity your cakes are so light, Veronica.'

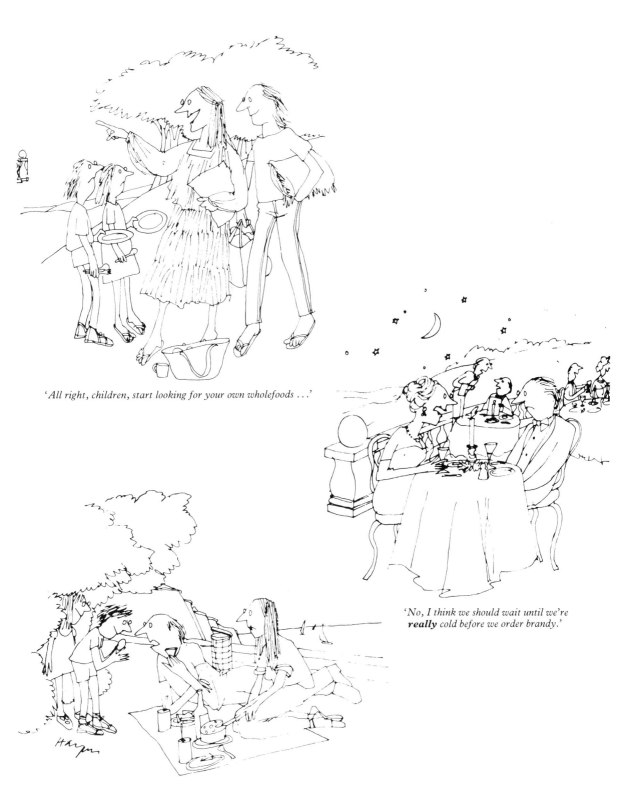

'All right, children, start looking for your own wholefoods ...'

'No, I think we should wait until we're **really** cold before we order brandy.'

'Yes, I would definitely think that hard-boiled egg has been deserted by its owner.'

Michael Bywater

YOGHURT

I am as susceptible to the lures of the flesh as all the rest of you. As all the rest of you put together, as a matter of fact. But there are some things which will not do. Take, for example, the entrancing sight of, oh gosh, let's have a change, one of those fine-boned incandescent redheads, alabaster skin, all Tintoretto and hands like eggshell with the blue veins showing through.

Then you lean closer and encounter horrors. Crust upon the blushing lips, and a sort of opaline scummy dribble slithering around the corners of the mouth; a frightful slippery exudate, with strands in, manifesting a hateful sort of semi-cheesiness and at the same time an abominable glistening, as of something which ought to be inside the body and not seen.

One knew that French women had a taste for the stuff, but now even English women, nice respectable sheilas with Aunts and things, may be seen putting the stuff in their mouths and even swallowing it, for heaven's sake, and some of them look as if they are enjoying the experience (though not many).

Yoghurt is one of those things one cannot understand, which is tolerated simply because it advertises its true nastiness. What I mean is, if you ordered milk and found this stuff floating on the top, you would send it back. 'This,' you would cry, 'has gone off. It is rotten.' 'No, no, no,' they would reply, 'it is the lactobacillus Bulgaricus, which ...' 'Yes!' you would respond. 'We know what the Bulgar gave rise to! Take this foul cheesiness away and swill it to the hogs which roll in mud and are as unspeakable as their vile food, and they will consume it with relish, smacking their lips!'

Yet christen it 'Yoghurt' – what a silly name – and tell people *exactly* what it is going to be like, and how it got to be like that, by being inoculated with disease and stored in conditions carefully controlled to remain at precisely the temperature and humidity conducive to specialised decay (and can you imagine what the Health and Safety scrivelsbies would say if you stored anything else in those conditions?) and gulls will flock to buy the stuff.

It is said to be healthy.

It is said that the peasants of Georgia live to be thousands of years old because they 'eat' this stuff. It is not true. They live to be very old indeed because they are desperately hanging on to life, hoping that something else will turn up which they can actually bear to eat. Nor are these skinny hateful creatures you see jogging around in fluorescent towelling incontinence suits 'fit' because of yoghurt. What they are is *thin*, because they poison their tastebuds with the awful products of mammary decay and have thus no healthy appetite for their grub, which would round them out, with womanly hips, some stature and female form, and norks like bloody footballs.

It was not always like this. In the old days, if you brought, for example, one's Mama a pot of glistening yoghurt you would have had it shoved up your nose pretty damned quickly, accompanied by a colourful imperious oath. Mama, in common with many of us, discovered yoghurt on the Côte d'Azur in 1959, the same year in which she was introduced to Naturism on the Ile de Levant. Kept her bathing costume on, of course, nor would she touch a drop of the stuff, but has had trouble with her back ever since; which shows that it is like radiation, an insidious force borne on the breeze to get in amongst you and sod things up.

They have it the wrong way round, the boffins. Since Chernobyl, a yoghurt lake has filled up because people are scared of contamination. I cannot see that, where yoghurt is concerned, a little glowing in the dark makes any difference.

They should be testing plutonium for yoghurt contamination. That is where the danger lies. In a different sort of society you could get vaccinated against the contagion but we are prey to it, victims, mere pot-fodder, watching for the symptoms: a spring in the step, a sparkle in the teeth, a twinkle in the eye, a stain on the chin and a swelling black boil in the armpit.

I am no paranoid but I detect a conspiracy. The colours which the mess comes in. Where else can you get heliotrope food? And the bits and lumps and strings and inexplicable pips and fibres which either lurk like beastly jam at the bottom or are commingled; and the lids which open at precisely the right velocity and angle to shoot a preliminary blob, a kind of warning shot, of the contents stickily on to your chin, or tie. These things are not accidental. Yoghurt reserves are being moved in by hostile forces, the same people, I expect, who encouraged those abominable vulgarians called Accurist to advertise on the Speaking Clock.

The stuff is building up. Are we to keep silence? Not on your Nellie. First decent day we get, there could be a meltdown. Something must be done. Free spoons and irradiated frootie-splodge yoghurt to all the baby-food lesbian feminist vegetarian anti-nuclear loonies and camp followers in local government. Just what they want. Yum yum yum.

May 1986

'They said, "You'll never succeed in that parish." They said, "You'll never make an impression on that tight-lipped bunch of Puritans." They said, "You'll never find the key to the wine cupboard." Well, two out of three ain't bad.'

James Ainsworth

divulges the secret ingredients of wine

DESIGNER LABELS

I have a bottle of red Burgundy dated 1892. It doesn't look it: the label is clean and modern and, peering at the colour through the punt, the wine appears no more than, say, four years old. I came by it last year, not at an expensive auction, but whilst traipsing round a *négociant*'s cellar. It cost no more than a few francs.

Of course, it's easy for a printer to make such a simple transposition of two figures, and the mistake was doubtless left uncorrected because nobody could possibly be fooled into thinking that it might be ninety years older than it is. But in other circumstances such apparent innocence could easily be misconstrued, because innocence is the last thing one associates with winemakers. They are normally at least one jump ahead of the law, and more often three.

The point of a label is threefold: to look pretty, comply with the law, and disclose as little information as possible. Italy wins hands down for looks, but there is stiff competition for secrecy, especially when compared with other products. 'Sugar, vegetable fat, butter, natural stabiliser, E412, natural flavouring,' volunteers my yoghourt pot, being careful to stress that these are '100% natural ingredients', whatever that means.

'Produce of France,' says the wine label in front of me. It gives me the château name, vouchsafes it as the place of bottling, records the year, and confirms that the wine is Appellation Haut-Médoc Contrôlée. But not a word about what's in it, not a mention of grapes. Nor indeed of any of the twenty or so additives that the EEC permits, and still less any reference to the ones it doesn't.

Were wine labels to come clean and reveal all, the bottles would be covered in paper.

The reason is simply that Nature is not such a punctilious wine-maker as we would like. Occasionally, Her Plan works like a dream: the grapes ripen without suffering from rot or being attacked by pests; oxygen doesn't get to the must and spoil it; the fermentation proceeds at the right temperature and speed; the wine falls bright naturally, without any protein haze or metal casse; no yeasts or bacteria remain in the finished wine, so the bottles don't explode. But for the most part, wine-makers assume that if anything can go wrong, it will, and they are entitled to take steps to prevent it.

The philosophy calls for basic hygiene measures to ensure that, at the very least, the grapes are healthy and the wine is biologically stable. What the law does is to recommend maximum levels, and codes of practice. Sprays must not be applied to the vines within the last few weeks before picking, in order that they will have a sporting chance of being washed off by the rain; only a certain amount of SO_2, the wine-maker's Dettol, can be added to keep the wine fresh and prevent it from oxidising.

It is further recognised that Nature is totally unreliable and keeps changing Her mind. One year, or in some areas, there is not enough natural acidity in the grapes, so an acidifier such as tartaric acid needs to be added; the next, or in another region, She provides too much, calling for a dip into the bag marked de-acidifier, or more likely potassium tartrate, potassium bicarbonate, or simply chalk. Then, in Germany and northern France, there may well have been an undersight, sunshinewise; if so, a few bags of sugar lobbed in before fermentation will bump up the alcohol level by the required degree or two. Where would the French beet sugar industry be if *vignerons* didn't take up their annual whack of 25,000 tons?

And so on. Sorbic acid, ascorbic acid (vitamin C), cultivated yeasts, yeast nutrient, tannin, carbon dioxide, potassium bitartrate, dried ox-blood, isinglass from the sturgeon's bladder, gelatine, casein, kaolin, silicon dioxide, pectinolytic enzymes, bentonite, pine resin. It's all there in EEC Regulation three three seven stroke seven nine, annex three. And in a lot of wines.

For the Fraud Squad, that bit's easy. Any fool with a gas chromatograph can check whether or not the levels have been exceeded. After that is where the tricky bit starts. In what is obviously a struggle to come to terms with bent wine-makers, Fritz Hallgarten in *Wine Scandal* (Weidenfeld & Nicolson) distinguishes two different kinds of mucking about. There is plain, straight-forward jiggery-pokery, such as adding diethylene glycol to increase body and sweet-ness, as a few Austrians did; or more seri-ously methanol to produce more alcohol, as one or two Italians did. On the assumption that pride goes before a scandal I should watch France next, since cheeky notices have been stuck up behind the sales counters at some co-operatives: 'Don't take risks, drink French wines.' They have obviously elected to forget such monumental cheating as the adulteration or false labelling of three million litres of Bordeaux wine, brought to light in 1974.

The other deceit is 'legalised fraud'. One may be forgiven for thinking, for instance, that a French or German wine with 1985 emblazoned across it must contain nothing but 1985 wine. Not so. It is legally entitled to contain 15% of wine from another year. (And from 15% it is but a short step to as much as you like and who's to know.) The German-sounding *Sekt* is allowed to come from Italy and have its sweetening of süss-reserve, and of course its Gothic-style label, added in Germany.

But all this is as nothing compared to what passes for wine-making in the land of the Rising Sun. Not that the Japanese do any-thing illegal. In fact, it is quite impossible to do anything illegal because they have no laws or labelling regulations to transgress. Thus it was last year that Austrian diethylene glycol managed to turn up in wines 'estate-bottled in Japan'. Furthermore, 'one hapless victim of the crossfire,' noted Hugh Johnson, 'was Australia. Very few Japanese seem to realise that Austria and Australia are two different countries – and even then they can't pro-nounce the difference.'

The acceptable face of 'law-free' zones is in the New World. Rather in the manner that Peter Ustinov claimed to have risen rapidly to the top of his profession because he didn't have qualifications to detain him at the bottom, so the absence of cumbersome do's and dont's leaves Californians and Australians free to make wine however they like (which, generally speaking, is splen-didly) and to write an essay on the back label giving temperature at date of picking, wind speed and direction, the names and addresses of everybody who helped, and throw in a couple of scientific formulae for good measure. As for the front, it only remains for us to get used to the sometimes less than elegant names: Bogle, Cakebread, Duck-horn, Schug, Wirra Wirra and Yalumba.

The most frightening information of all that a label might, but doesn't, divulge, is where the money goes. Compared to 'addi-tives' such as Duty, VAT, bottling, delivery and overheads, the original cost of the wine can be disgustingly small. A line inscribed around a bottle selling for £2.50 would show that the wine accounts for approximately a quarter of the total; if there are two of you drinking, that would represent about three-quarters of a glass each. Or as much as would fit into a small yoghourt pot.

July 1986

Cyril Ray

GOOD HEALTH

.

Off and on during the war, and for a few years afterwards, I rented rooms from an old cock known to gossip-writers – but not to anyone else I ever heard of – as the Squire of Piccadilly. He had been born in the year of the Mutiny, attended Disraeli's funeral, and been too old to be commissioned, as he used to say he had wished, in the fifty thousand horse and foot going to Table Bay in 1899.

He was 93 when, in 1950, his manservant (oh yes, he had a manservant, nearly as old as himself) came to my door, bearing with due reverence a bottle of the Cockburn 1908 – my own birthdate, and a great year not only for people but for port. 'Mr Stone knows you like a glass of wine, sir, and he's been told by his doctor to give up port, so he's giving his cellar away.'

I have wondered for 35 years whether, had he said pooh to the doctor and 'another glass' to his man, Willie Stone would not have lived, as he did, to the age of 101 and three-quarters, or whether another little drink wouldn't have done him any harm for those remaining nine years. And, if it didn't, whether those nine years might have been happier ones. I shall never know.

Nor have I ever decided whether it is better to be fit and fractious off the bottle or happy and unhealthy on – a lack of decision that results only (according to my loved ones) in my being both fuddled *and* fractious.

Having had a rabbi ancestor, a more recent but still remote early upbringing at the hands of Lancashire Wesleyans, and being as it were rurally diaconal by marriage, my first instincts were to seek oracular advice by the *sortes biblicae*, and a fat lot of use the Good Book is to one of troubled mind. Wine is a mocker, strong drink is raging, saith Solomon – but is this a blanket admonition, or is he drawing a distinction between the mere giggles induced by burgundy, say, or champagne, and the horrors brought on by the hard stuff? A little wine, Paul told Timothy, for his stomach's sake, but never mind Tim's tum, what about my liver?

Turning from revealed religion to the miraculous discoveries of modern science, I find in the pages of *Wine, Health and Society, the Proceedings of a Symposium Sponsored by the University of California, the Society of the Medical Friends of Wine and the Wine Institute of San Francisco*, held in November 1981, that so far as my liver is concerned much depends on the kinetics of ethanol absorption, which in turn is conditioned by the reoxidation of NADH, which occurs chiefly in the microchrondia and the flavoprotein cytochrome system. The acetate is translocated from the liver and is oxidized extrahepatically. The reactions for the NAD system may, as perhaps will already have occurred to you, be summarized by the following:

$$C_2H_5OH + NAD \xrightarrow{ADH} CH_3CHO - NADH$$

$$CH_3CHO + NADH \xrightarrow{AldDH} + CH_3COOH + NAD$$

– a mnemonic that somehow escapes me whenever a bottle of gin heaves into sight.

People do go on about one's liver, but what about spontaneous combustion, eh? Dickens is more alarming than all those California doctors put together, if one recalls the fate of Mr Krook, Lord Chancellor of the Rag and Bottle shop in *Bleak House*, 'continually in liquor', of whom nothing is left after a carouse too many save a 'smouldering vapour in the room, and a dark greasy coating on the walls and ceiling ... call the death by any name ... it is the same death eternally – inborn, inbred, engendered in the corrupted humours of the vicious body itself, and that only – Spontaneous Combustion, and none other of all the deaths that can be died.'

It turns the stomach – pass the brandy ...

Let us topers turn to happier happenings. Tokay Essenz is made in the far north-east of Hungary, from grapes that have been shrivelled into concentrated sweetness by the 'noble rot' that also informs such great sauternes as Yquem, individually picked and allowed to let drip their juice, without being pressed, but simply under their own weight. This clear, golden, intensely honey-sweet wine is credited with all sorts of therapeutic, not to mention aphrodisiac, qualities. It is said indeed that, applied to the lips of a dying man, it will restore him to life.

In my modest cellar there is a half-litre bottle apiece for my wife, my son and me, against our respective appointed days – not that we believe in these old babushkas' tales but in the pure spirit of scientific curiosity. So it was with Raymond Postgate, as sceptical as a man could be, but who bade his family have a bottle handy, and let's see ... When, with the end nigh, the wine was duly applied, he did not, alas, come back to life but, the family later told me, he died not only with the Tokay Essenz on his lips, but with a smile.

The learned Mrs M. F. K. Fisher, the Elizabeth David of the United States, in her little book, *A Cordiall Water*, 'a garland of odd and old receipts to assuage the ills of man and beast', recommended 'gin for women's monthly misery.' 'Gin is our best friend, girl,' a fellow sufferer informed me soberly in a coal town in southern Illinois. 'It's not the liquor in it, it's the juniper juice that does the trick.'

But among what she calls her 'cure-alls', suitable for both sexes and all ages, 'the simplest of all,' she says, 'and the most all-embracing, is what in France is called 'a little slice of ham' .... a little slice of which, especially when taken in bed with a glass of good wine, will cure completely or at least help cure exhaustion, migraine, grippe, gout, disappointment in love, business worries, childbed fever, dizziness, coughing, and indeed almost everything else except Death and Taxes.'

People who follow this prescription, says Mrs Fisher, 'will not suffer from indigestion. Their livers will not shrivel in one last paroxysm of revulsion before the dainty fat slice of embalmed pork-flesh, and the salted pickles, and the mildly alcoholic flushing of the fermented grape juice. They will not, in other words, die.'

'(*Then.*)'

There are those, I know, who keep brandy in the house purely for medicinal reasons, and very sensible, too. Vyvyan Holland, who survived the cruel indignities he suffered as a child for being the son of Oscar Wilde to become the kindest and most civilised of men, once told me of a great-uncle who used to keep a few rare bottles of fine old cognac for special friends. Came a day when his house took fire, and one particular fireman behaved with exceptional courage. The old gentleman offered him a glass of his oldest and finest in grateful tribute, upon which the fireman, drenched by the hoses, took off boots and socks, saying, 'A very happy thought, sir, and thank you kindly. I'm a teetotaller myself, but there's nothing like brandy for stopping a cold,' and poured the golden glory over his feet.

July 1985

ffolkes

THE CURE

Drunks should not be arrested but sent to a drying-out centre, says a Government report.

ffolkes investigates.

'You're improving, Finnegan, that makes twenty-f
minutes without your elbow moving.'

'If you're good they'll let you drink champagne
out of Matron's shoe.'

'Dammit, Battersby, whose side are you on?'

'Doctor, come quickly! They're operating an illicit still
in the Brendan Behan Ward!'

'He says that he's absolutely cured and that we can
keep the rabbit.'

Alan Coren

TABLE TORQUE

Last year, 953,000 Guardian readers visited a restaurant.

The Guardian

'Justin, Miranda, hallo, sorry we're late, we had a hell of a job finding a bicycle for Lok Nol Phung, then he fell off on Primrose Hill and a borzoi savaged him. This is Lok, I think we mentioned him, he's a boatperson, we got him through Belsize Action Now.'

'Hallo, Lok, I'm Justin, this is Miranda, welcome to Canonbury, I hope you like Turkish food.'

'He doesn't speak any English, Justin, but don't worry, he eats anything, they were off Borneo for nine weeks with nothing but biscuits.'

'Are you sure he's a genuine refugee, Pippa?'

'Oh for God's sake, Miranda!'

'Well, I *have* heard that something like eighty per cent of them aren't Vietnamese at all, the Vietnamese don't have the cash, the ones that get out are mostly Chinese pimps, that kind of thing, dope pedlars. I'm only mentioning it.'

'Bloody hell, Miranda, do you realise what we went through to get him? The FCO and Home Office bores I had to stuff at the Connaught, people I hadn't seen since Millfield, my God, there were moments when I found myself thinking: If I have to listen to one more bloody account of David Owen's personal habits, I shall chuck up this whole business and get a Filipino couple instead!'

'May I suggest to Madame that Monsieur do the ordering? Otherwise there
may be incalculable harm to Monsieur's self-image.'

'Have you told her yet?'

'Virtually.'

'What?'

'She's not feeling very well lately. I've given her a pretty strong impression, though. Is there any chance your flatmate's going to be out picketing Mothercare again tonight?'

'What sort of strong impression?'

'We've talked about my forty-third birthday a lot. About how there ought to be more to life than the Criminal Bar.'

'Oh Christ!'

'No, really, she's forming a pretty clear idea. When I suggested that she enrolled in that furniture restoring class at the Northern Poly, I honestly sensed she recognised that I was trying to edge her towards being self-supporting.'

'*When* will you tell her?'

'She may have a lump.'

'I beg your pardon?'

'You seem to have bent your fork. I'm rather banking on it turning out to be a polyp, of course. But it might be a lump.'

'I think I'll go now.'

'Hang on, let's finish our chateaubriand first, I mean, God knows, darling, I'm as keen as you are, ha-ha-ha, but when I think of all those poor little buggers starving in Ethiopia, I think it is, the idea of ten quidsworth of steak, not including bloody veg, just being left on the . . .'

'You finish it.'

'Oh, hell, do sit down, Tamsin, there's a junior from my bloody chambers over there, look, I'll tell you what I'll do, I'll get her to

'How good to know that, if really pushed, one can produce one's own artificial colouring.'

see someone *privately*, I mean you know how much that goes against everything I believe in, but at least it'll speed things up a bit, doesn't that *prove* how important our relationship is to ...'

'Waitperson!'

'Sir?'

'Don't call him sir. He doesn't want you to call him sir, do you, Freddie?'

'Oh Lord, no!'

'If you called him sir, Florence Nightingale would have thrown herself under the King's horse in vain, wouldn't she, Freddie?'

'A lamp trampled for nothing, Germaine.'

'Are you ready to order, er?'

'Call him Freddie. Yes, he is. Or, rather, I am. He'll have the *cojones con arroz*.'

'And for you, madame?'

'Nothing for me. I'll just watch.'

'I think it's wonderful to have a restaurant overlooking the Grand Union Canal. It's a complete, as it were, breakthrough. It means Tristram and I can eat out. We only travel by canal. Tristram worked for some years to develop a wooden bicycle, but it came to nothing. We won't go near anything steel, ultimately they're all defence nexus spin-offs, aren't they? As for shoes, it's either the skin of some poor fellow-being, or else it's some oil-derived polymer artefact torn from the womb of Mother Earth. Wood is all right if the tree fell down naturally, but then it tends to be wormy, and Tristram had as little success with clogs as he had with the bicycle. So we go barefoot; apart from all the other advantages, you never crush anything live without being aware that a little light has gone out somewhere, reminding you of the Great Chain that links us all. We wove our barge out of dead rattan, it's marvellous provided you remember not to get out of your depth. The canals will all be back someday, you know. Tristram hopes to be able to pull us from Islington to Stonehenge by Walpurgisnacht 1990, don't you, darling? Do try their chickweed soufflé, it's a shattering psychic experience.'

'Our daily's been battered, you know. It's

TRUE HUMILITY
Right Reverend Host. 'I'M AFRAID YOU'VE GOT A BAD EGG, MR JONES!'
The Curate. 'OH NO, MY LORD, I ASSURE YOU! PARTS OF IT ARE EXCELLENT!'

the great boon of living in Parliament Hill Fields, Kentish Town is close enough for one to be kept *engaged*. I mean, Gareth has never seen anyone even remotely battered at the agency, and the closest I've come to it at the boutique was when a gay flyweight came in to buy some Third World dress studs for his manager.'

'It's not too different in Hampstead, is it, Charles? We saw a Soviet Jew outside Jack Straw's Castle last Sunday. I mean, he wasn't battered, of course, but he was terribly gaunt.'

'Oh, come on, Fiona, I mean, our daily has had three *teeth* knocked out, for God's sake, and she's talked to me about it, face to face, hasn't she, Gareth? *As a person I know!*'

'It's true, Fiona, she actually had the teeth in her purse, I saw them. We brought Caleb,

Goneril and even little Xavier in to see them, too. I think that if you're going to educate children privately, in this year of grace 1979, you owe it to them not to cut them off entirely from society's realities. After all, they must know what's what: as soon as the *immediate* educational crisis is over, as soon as they've got the bugs out of the comprehensive system, we're going to have them state-educated.'

'Oh, so are we!'
'So are we!'
'So are we!'

'You'll like it here. The chef was in Parkhurst for ages. How's your radio play coming along?'

'Fortunately, we've found someone to run

A DIFFICULT CONUNDRUM
'HI, WAITER, WHAT DO YOU CALL THIS?' 'BEAN SOUP, SIR.'
'YES, IT'S BEEN SOUP, BUT WHAT THE DOOCE IS IT NOW?'

our play-group. A super girl, couple of years ago she thought she was developing a pulmonary embolism as the result of taking the pill, so she became a lesbian until they come up with a low-irritant coil. Her brother's in the Maze and she's saving up for a gun.'

'Is he a prisoner of conscience?'

'Oh, God yes! He lies awake all night torturing himself for not having opened the bags before they left the bank, all they got away with was two million deposit slips.'

'How appalling! I'll just bet that bank has investments in South Africa.'

'And how much of *that* does the grey seal see?'

'Quite. I say, Pru, you're a wonderfully aware and caring person! Would you, could we, might it, oh, hell, what I'm trying to say is, have you ever thought about becoming a two-parent family?'

January 1979

Michael Bateman

ON DELICATESSENS

How is it that so many foreigners and immigrants who come to our country do not appreciate wholesome English food?

Britain leads the world in food technology. We pioneered a form of bread which dispensed with the tough crust, such a threat to tender teeth: a bread which stayed moist and fresh (or seemed so) for a whole week, remaining soft and spongey; a bread in which our scientists overcame the problem of uneven baking flavour by giving it none at all.

Has this been appreciated by the Germans and Italians and French and Poles and Hungarians who crowd our shores? No, it has not. They seek out foreign food shops and delicatessens and buy hard, dark loaves with the pungent smell of wholewheat and rye and other flours, baked in so many shapes and sizes that no two appear, or taste, alike; some so dense that you could hardly call them bread, like pumpernickel; some so airy and fairy that they vanish in your mouth, like Jewish *cholla*.

Another strange thing about these foreigners. They have no comprehension of the work we have done in creating the definitive sausage, outstanding in its place in the world. It has taken 70 years – and two world wars – to take this crude mixture of minced pork, and develop it into the bland and inoffensive product it is today, a mixture of pulverised pork fat and harmless cereal filler; something that many vegetarians could eat without too much conscience.

Our visiting friends are to be seen crowding into delicatessens, where large and rude sausages hang sweating, some nearly the size of a woman wrestler's thighs, others obscene little coils; white, yellow, brown, red, black; their ends cut off to show a marbling of fat; with no clue as to what animal they might be made from. The British pork sausage is as safe as the Union Jack. Can you say the same of such unlikely aliens as knackwurst, kockwurst, and knoblauchworst; bluckworst, bockworst and bratwurst; kabanos and krakowska; salami, salchichon, salpicão, butifara and longaniza; pinkel and plockwurst?

Furthermore, they fail to recognise the convenience and ease of English cheese; the way it is wrapped to confine its odours inside transparent plastic skin, so that finger, and nose, may be protected hygienically from taint.

What these foreigners do is seek out, in their delicatessens, cheeses with smells which reach out to grab you. They prod each one with their forefinger, till they find one that gives in the middle. They make sure it is moist and supple, on the point of becoming runny. Sometimes they'll ask to try a piece, then lick their fingers clean. Cheeses like smelly, veined gorgonzola, Bel Paese, Provolone, Parmesan, Dolcelatte; St Paulin, Pont l'Évêque, Roblochon, voluptuous and yellow; or soft white cheeses of sheep's milk, like Banon, or cheeses made from goat's milk, chèvre, soft and creamy and crumbly; harsh, hard, and salty.

The fish in these shops are not proper English fish, frozen rectangles, of equal size, contained in plastic and cardboard to remove all sense of fishiness: but instead in all the natural shapes of the sea. Smoked sides of salmon, herring smoked, salted, pickled, often with wine and spices. Even the beans do not come in cans, as they should, but in dozens of different kinds of bags, usually unlabelled, with no clue to identity or means of cooking them.

The delly was born in America in the 1890's of immigrant European parentage. The shops were usually Jewish, and the delicacies they sold were for eating on the premises or for taking away: as in *pastrami on rye, to go*. They married into Britain's foreign food shops, and by the Fifties their children were spreading outwards from Soho, across the country. No threat to the supermarket which today, unable to beat them, tries to join them. Be warned, though. The supermarket is no more than a shop which sells food.

The delicatessen at its best offers the heady excitement of travel, the tension of crossing into another culture and experiencing it.

In an English supermarket, products are seductively wrapped. Packets are designed by the best-paid artists at the most skilful advertising agencies. Millions of pounds go into making food look good, not only on the shelves, but in magazines and on television;

they speak of its wholesomeness, goodness, its roots in tradition.

But in the delicatessen there is no need for this. The food speaks for itself. It needs no copywriter. Sometimes the staff speak up for it, with modesty and pride. Or they may even speak against it.

At a time when many shopkeepers despise the food they have to sell (and sometimes seem to despise the customers for buying it) the delicatessen is an anachronism. For instance, the mutual respect between shopkeeper and customer.

When my own local delicatessen is crowded, twenty of us trying to shove a way to the counter, forced against the wet side of a tub of olives, pushed into a pile of rye breads, dodging your face from a hanging bunch of garlic bulbs, all the assistants behind the counter will turn away from us to solve some sudden, minor problem.

This American lady wants smoked spare rib. 'Ah, they were delicious, I remember,' says the Pole, or the Hungarian, or the Czech. 'But there's no call for them in this country.' This is the cue for other contributions. They do have smoked belly of pork. A search of the shop, its back rooms, cellars, and storeplaces begins. We all wait till it's found; the lady wants a very *little* bit, she says. 'As little as you like, my love.'

Regrettably, when my turn comes, I do not get the same attention. I find it hard to come to terms with the disorganisation, the shouting, confusion, and on this day the slowness of the girl at the cheese counter. I have raised a knotty problem for her: I want a piece of cheese.

But I endure it. Because everything in the shop, perhaps several thousand items, has been sought out with love, care, and discrimination. It is sold with a fierce and protective pride. It is simply the best they can possibly get.

January 1980

Clement Freud

CUISINE PORTUGAISE

I took a villa in Portugal for Whitsun to finish my novel; I am a very slow reader. With the villa came a Maria. Marias are housekeepers that go with Portuguese villas; they are aged between 36 and 60, dark, silent, industrious, with dogs and a husband living within barking distance of the residence. The prospectus states: 'Maria does simple cooking.'

When I came, Maria had left a simple chicken with lemon in the oven. As this is by no means my first encounter with the species, I recognised it at once as one of the three well-known versions of chicken *à la Maria*.

The usual one is prepared by cutting a

lemon into thinnish slices, dotting them around a chicken, placing this on a roasting-tray, covering it with washing-up liquid and leaving it in a hot oven for one and a half hours. Then turn off oven, keeping chicken therein, to shrivel to kitchen temperature awaiting the arrival of the tenants. The second method is to cut the lemon into wedges; place these on and around the chicken and cook as before. The third and subtlest way is to cut one half of the lemon into slices, the other into segments. If there are other methods, I have yet to encounter them. If you don't like the taste of washing-up liquid, which is oil-coloured in Portugal, you should go elsewhere.

La cuisine portugaise is not one about which many have heard. Many were right. There is a lot of fish, which they grill; there are a lot of sardines which they grill for themselves and put into tins for the rest of the world; and the staple is salt cod which follows the Duke of York syndrome – except that instead of marching up the hill, and then down, they salt it for a month and then de-salt it for a week. What is left is nowhere near as nice as fish fingers.

If it were not for Portuguese dogs and Portuguese food and Portuguese roads, the country would be wholly desirable, give or take Portuguese estate agents who mass occupy premises, as do building societies in England. Like building societies, they all sell the same things at the same price and occupy the kind of sites that should house shops.

This means that you have trouble finding Portuguese bakers; the bread is good, the cakes – heavily influenced by the profusion of almonds, therefore marzipan – are all right if you care for that sort of thing, but as bread is cheap and houses expensive, food shops are in side streets. I had not considered that where bread and cakes are cheap, there is little home-baking and I spent much of my week trying to find flour and yeast. The former can be located in supermarkets on the unfashionable shelves, where ours sell shampoo. Yeast is unobtainable. Go into a baker's shop and ask for yeast and they look at you like they do in American massage parlours if you ask for a massage.

Tomatoes cost no more than 15p a pound and are the real Mediterranean breed; buy them green and on a good day they will be red by the time you get them home. What EEC tomato-growers will do about that when our oldest allies join the Common Market does not bear thinking about.

Figs are cheap and good: dried figs. Olive oil is available and cheaper than it is in Britain, and there are huge bunches of herbs that should persuade any reasonably ambitious housekeeper to make herb vinegars, and enable them to make sensational salad dressings for the sensational salad ingredients that abound. I wish countries would be proud of the fruit and vegetables that they grow superbly, instead of trying to emulate those that have talents in the butchery department. I shall say no more about their lamb other than to say it deserves the oily mass in which they cook it.

What I failed to find in the Algarve – though I recall many years ago at the Aziz Hotel in Lisbon, before the Revolution, eating the finest smoked swordfish I have ever tasted – was smoked fish. They have eels but none smoked; they have mackerel and trout-like varieties and fish that would pass for herrings. All are either grilled or baked with tomatoes and yuck.

Inspired by a Normandy market town's restaurant notice that said, 'We have what is probably the best fish soup in Europe, which means the world', I picked half a dozen unlikely looking fish in Albufeira market, boiled the heads and tails and bones and innards in water spiked with herbs and vinegar and onion, and after half an hour on the hob sieved $1\frac{1}{2}$ pints of the liquor into another pan and thickened it with two tablespoons each of tomato purée and flour, and a dessertspoon of saffron mustard. They did not sell fresh cream in the shops I visited, but for which the resultant soup really might have finished even higher up the totem pole of excellence.

Funny how the word 'soup' is almost a pejorative. Soup, they say, is a waste of good eating space. Ours is the only civilised language which skimps on syllables in gastronomy: soup, fish, meat, sweet. Fat, lard, oil. Peas, beans, sprouts. Beef, veal, pork, ham, lamb (mutton had an extra syllable and look what happened to mutton. Too much trouble to keep it alive). Cod, hake, skate – it is not till you get to the fashionable end of the range that you come across lob-ster, hal-i-but and salm-on.

The strange thing is that syllables upgrade: call a soup a consommé, a potage or a garbure, and people sit up and take notice; rename your stew a casserole or ragoût and it is appreciated. Under the name of chicken, cock and hen achieve respectability.

As if it were not hard enough to prepare decent food, you now have to be a philologist also, to make your trade respectable.

June 1985

*'At last, Harry. The recognition
we've fought for for years.'*

A. P. Herbert

RED BREAD

I never, never liked brown bread,
Whatever aunts and uncles said.
In vain they tried to make me see
This beastly food was good for me.

Though full of nourishment (said Nurse)
It looked like mud, and tasted worse;
And I would seldom care a lot
If things were good for me, or not.
(Yes, even at that early age
Foul Self-indulgence took the stage
And I would tend to sulk, or strike,
If barred from what I chanced to like.)
At all events, I laid it down
The bread I ate should *not* be brown.

Years passed: and other people sought
To make me eat as Britons ought.
'Brown bread' was pressed on me no more;
The 'whole-meal loaf' became the bore.
And though I liked the novel name
The stuff, I thought, was much the same.
Men saw me pleasantly engrossed
In bread-and-cheese or buttered toast,
And wondered how a man could eat
'De-naturized' anæmic wheat.
They said, for all the goodness there
One might as well consume a chair,
Fry bits of blotting-pad, or hat,
Or spread one's butter on the mat.
I answered 'Nature was not meant
To be a one-stringed instrument.
She plays for each a different tune,
E.g.' (I said) 'observe the moon
And how the tide is high elsewhere
When it's Low Water over there.'

I said that since the age of two
White bread had been the bread I knew,
And that, as far as I could see,
Was what was 'natural' for me.
At all events, I laid it down,
That bread I ate should *not* be brown.

But now, through Hitler and his works,
We find ourselves in other circs.
The Government, I understand,
Of our superb but sea-girt land
Are starting, just to win the war,
This prehistoric hare once more
And they desire us all to eat

This unattractive whole-meal wheat.
Well, more than anything, I love
To do the will of H.M. Gov.
I don't like Communists much more
Than, right or wrong, I did before.
But as I now salute the Red
So will I bow to dear brown bread
Because, as my wise rulers say,
We shall save tonnage in this way
(They say that half a million tons
Will thus be wrested from the Huns).
But let this point be understood –
No man must tell me it is good:
Nor shall I jump in girlish glee
If someone screams it's good for *me*.
My principles shall not be shed:
I say, *I do not like brown bread!*
I will attempt this awful thing
To save the sailors of the King;
I contemplate some loss of face
That we may have more cargo-space.
And you, I'm sure, for very shame
Will ultimately do the same.

But when we've put the Prussian down,
The bread I eat will *not* be brown.

August 1941

Adrian Robson

WHAT'S OFF IN LONDON

Exquisite solemnity.

'For two, señor?' Ignoring nodded acqui-escence, the head waiter glides ahead, as if on roller skates, showing the way. He averts his eyes in self-conscious pride, indicating a red-velvet cocooned recess.

'Very nice,' says Emma. Her smile dissolves into apprehension. 'What's that squeaking? You haven't got mice have you?'

'Forgive me señora. My roller skates, they need oiling.'

The band falls silent and the drummer begins a drum roll. The head waiter adjusts his shirt cuffs, looks his customers firmly in the eye, and with a flourish produces two menus from nowhere. The drummer's cymbals crash, and the band resumes its repertoire of vaguely familiar tunes.

Emma and Julian begin to study their menus. A rabbit's ear suddenly springs out of the head waiter's shirt front. 'Not yet,' he mutters pushing the ear back and buttoning the shirt.

'No, not yet,' says Julian, looking up and smiling. 'We'll be ready in a moment.'

'Señor,' the head waiter inclines his head and closes his eyes. He turns away in an attitude of unobtruding attentiveness.

'The service is always excellent here,' Julian confides to Emma as the head waiter struggles to push a rabbit's leg back into his shirt.

'I'd like a green salad without dressing or smirk!'

'I think we're ready to order now.' Julian looks up again, smiling.

'Señor,' says the waiter taking out a pen.

'The melon, would you recommend it?'

'Is very good today, señor, yes.'

'Good, well I think we'll start with melon then. Followed by haricots à la four flambés, and then, I think, lapin au naturel.'

'Si, señor. And some wine?'

'Yes. Red, I think; Campo Viejo 1970.'

The head waiter turns away and snaps his fingers imperiously. The wine waiter and two others come forward; a rabbit nose and rabbit whiskers pop through the head waiter's straining shirt front.

A small boy tugs at his mother's sleeve and points excitedly.

'Fame can be a little embarrassing sometimes.' Julian examines his finger nails with a tired sigh.

'A small price to pay for success.' Emma gazes at his noble forehead.

'Get back,' hisses the head waiter clasping his hands across his bulging stomach. 'Not you,' he says as the waiters retreat in fear. He hands them the order and glides haughtily away. A mouse peeps out from his trouser leg squeaking with delight.

The small boy's mother whispers to her son, who returns downcast to his soup with only the occasional surreptitious glance across the room.

'Ah, the melon,' says Julian. 'It does look excellent don't you think?' He tastes the wine and nods approval.

A waiter wheels a trolley to their table. He makes sure the arrangement of its contents is meticulous: spoons, forks, pepper and salt, various bottles, a highly polished portable burner. He disappears momentarily, returning with a large oval silver dish. The edge is artistically decorated with leaves of lettuce, finely sliced tomato and cucumber and two pink rosebuds; in the centre, delicately placed among the lettuce leaves, a tin of baked beans. He holds out the dish for Julian's inspection: 'Yes, that looks fine, thank you.'

'All right. Last offer. Two bread and fish for a cheese and chutney!'

A second waiter brings forward a wicker basket containing a large white loaf, its tasteful red and white wrapper intact.

'It is medium sliced?' says Julian.

'Si señor.' The waiter draws himself up, a little offended.

'Thank you, that's fine. It's always as well to check these things,' Julian explains confidentially to Emma. They begin slicing into their melon as the waiters withdraw behind the trolley.

The head waiter returns and casts an expert eye over the preparations.

'Matches.' He holds out his hand; one of the waiters gives him a box of matches. The burner lights with a bang, adding to the sense of occasion. Diners peer across the room, guessing to their companions what dish has been chosen for this couple's evening of celebration, declaring with an air of superior gastronomic experience what they would have had if it had been them.

The head waiter now pulls out an elegant dark wood chopping board, a long slender knife which glints in the candle light. The loaf of bread is set vertically on the wood and with four deft strokes the crust and wrapper are severed from the body of the loaf, which is turned faster than the eye can see after each stroke of the blade.

The crusts and wrapper are tossed into the lower part of the trolley, and with a swift movement the loaf is turned on its side and the remaining crust and paper are removed from the ends.

Flicking through the slices – the head waiter's experience of dealing cards in a casino stands him in good stead – he selects two: those with the most aesthetically pleasing arrangement of holes caused by trapped air in the baking. The rest of the slices are discarded and the two whose excellence has set them apart are placed on a long oval serving dish.

'This is the bit I like.' Emma, finishing her melon, pushes the plate away, and watches in delight as the head waiter sprinkles alcohol from various bottles over the slices of bread.

'I don't know how they always manage to get the quantities just right,' says Julian, who believes in giving credit where due.

A lapine muzzle seizes a lettuce leaf as the head waiter leans across the trolley waving the serving dish in the direction of the burner. Orange and blue flames engulf the bread as Julian smiles magnanimously at Emma, and the head waiter straightens his shirt front.

'What's that crunching noise?' Emma is perplexed. 'It sounds like a squad of soldiers marching on gravel, but it seems to be coming from your shirt.'

The head waiter bares his teeth at Emma and examines the ceiling out of the corner of his eye. An air of expectation and unspoken 'Well?'s.

'Is my stomach. I was in the army an' my stomach gets nostalgia. Please, no interruptions now. Is the difficult part. Opener please.' A waiter hands him a short-bladed tin opener.

'They still do it in the traditional way,' explains Julian. 'None of your rotary tin openers for the cognoscenti.'

One of the waiters sidles up to Julian. 'I once 'ad a Cognoscenti 450. Terrible car. Like you say, she just like a rotary tin opener. The gears fall out ofter 4,000 kilometres.'

Head waiter attacking the tin with a thrusting motion, ejecting its contents through jagged edges into a copper pan set above the flame.

'Why is that waiter handing him a sticky plaster?' asks Emma.

'Tradition,' Julian explains. 'In the olden days a lot of people used to cut themelves on the tins.' They watch as he wraps it symbolically round the index finger of his right hand.

By now the flames are dying away on the plate of bread, leaving the two slices a fashionable shade of charcoal grey. The con-

Applicant (for situation as Parlour-maid). 'SHOULD I BE EXPECTED TO HAND THINGS AT LUNCH, MADAM, *OR DO YOU STRETCH?*'

tents of the copper pan are poured onto the toasted bread and the head waiter stands back allowing an underling to serve the two portions to the couple. He folds his hands across his stomach, an artist surveying his creation with pride. Rabbit's teeth seize a finger and blood spurts down his white shirt.

'Tomato sauce,' says Julian knowledgeably as the head waiter retreats to the kitchens. 'All part of the tradition.'

They have barely finished the second course when the head waiter returns looking smug. He is carrying a top hat in a hand now bandaged with two sticky plasters. A portly under-waiter follows him at a trot. The head waiter catches the eye of the band leader who points his baton meaningfully at the drummer.

A drum roll starts as the rest of the band falls silent. Bowing, the head waiter shows the inside of the top hat first to Julian and Emma, then to the rest of the diners.

'Nothing inside,' Julian mouthes helpfully to the audience as the drum roll gets louder.

With a swift movement the head waiter seizes a pair of rabbit ears and holds triumphantly aloft a rabbit wearing a blue ribbon round its neck. Cymbals crash as he pushes the rabbit into the top hat, struggling to free its toes from a button hole. Waiters and diners break into wild cheering and polite clapping respectively. Handing the top hat to the portly under-waiter, the head waiter bows deeply.

A second drum roll drowns the small boy's cry of 'It was in his shirt' and the subsequent muffled noises he makes when a nearby waiter deftly inserts a large doughnut in his mouth. A second pair of rabbit ears mysteriously appear in the head waiter's hand as he takes the top hat from the under-waiter. This time a pink ribbon round the rabbit's neck. The hat containing the two rabbits is placed on the table as the drummer crashes the cymbals and the band breaks into a double speed version of 'Run, Rabbit, Run'.

Two waiters step forward and put before Julian and Emma two plates elegantly garnished with a salad of lettuce, tomatoes, green and red peppers, onions and cucumber. The head waiter carefully takes one rabbit from the hat and places it in the centre of Emma's plate where it crouches suspiciously. The second rabbit jumps out of the hat and crawls with a bored expression onto Julian's plate. The band plays a long and strident chord which dissolves into an unobtrusive and almost tuneless version of 'Raindrops keep falling on my head'.

'Oh, Julian.' Emma gazes deeply into his eyes.

He reaches across the table and covers Emma's hand with his own. 'Something special for a special occasion.'

'It's ... it's very ... unusual,' Emma falters over her choice of words.

'Special,' insists Julian.

'You know, I'm not sure that I can eat any more, after all the courses we've already had,' says Emma. 'I think I'll just have a little of the salad.'

The rabbit with the blue ribbon has already had the same idea.

'Damn rabbit's eaten all the salad.' Julian looks round indignant for a waiter. Emma looks for a waiter too.

The blue-ribboned rabbit, finishing off the lettuce, notices the other rabbit which starts twitching nervously, then leaps off the table and is chased by the blue-ribboned rabbit into the kitchens.

A waiter appears at last. 'You finish already? Ah, you leave the salad. We men, we don't spoil the taste with the lettuce, eh? Is the women who always got to have their bits of lettuce, eh? Anything for sweet?'

May 1977

'And the egg and chips to follow.'

E. S. Turner

RISE AND SHINE

'Hope is a good breakfast,' said Francis Bacon, a pathetic observation from a man with a name like that. But, the way things are going, hope will soon be the main constituent of the British breakfast; or; if not hope, quiet desperation. Already, according to the Man from Sainsbury's, one British adult in five eats no breakfast at all.

Only 18 per cent of us, it seems, demand a cooked breakfast, compared with 50 per cent 20 years ago; and 25 per cent settle for bread or toast. Of the rest, many have taken to browsing on bran, yoghurt, muesli and other alien belly-liners.

So much for the Great British Breakfast of legend, the empire-builder's meal, the meal which the condemned man devoured 'heartily' on his way to the gallows, the meal for which British Rail now charges £4.50, no doubt in a frantic attempt to kill it off.

The Man from Sainsbury's maintains that, as a tradition, the Great British Breakfast dates only from the 1920s. Well, it all depended on your social status. In these pages, in 1924, A. P. H. carolled:

O breakfast! O breakfast! The meal of my heart!

Bring porridge, bring sausage, bring fish for a start.

Bring kidneys and mushrooms and partridges' legs,

But let the foundation be bacon and eggs.

Do not suppose that 'partridges' legs' was introduced merely to rhyme with eggs. Sir Winston Churchill was rumoured to eat a covey of partridges for breakfast (whereas his chum Sir Alexander Korda settled for cold duck, *pâté de foie gras*, salami and beer).

But, when Sir Alan Herbert wrote, bacon and eggs had long been the foundation of the middle-class breakfast.

In her first *Book of Household Management*, in 1861, Mrs Beeton has only half a page (out of 1,112) on 'the comfortable meal called breakfast'. Desirable hot dishes include broiled mackerel, whiting and herrings, dried haddocks, mutton chops, rump steaks, kidneys, sausages and, of course, bacon and eggs. The cold dishes on the sideboard comprise 'collared and potted meats or fish, cold game or poultry, veal-and-ham pies, game and rumpsteak pies, ham, tongue &c.' All with toast, muffins and marmalade.

As an afterthought, almost, Mrs Beeton says that in summer strawberries are particularly refreshing at breakfast, 'as also grapes or even currants'. The citrous breakfast was yet to come; jokes about people squirting each other in the eye with new-fangled grapefruit date, roughly, from the 1920s.

How much of any given spread was one expected to eat? There is a clue in a breakfast menu from HMS *Ophir*, in 1901, shortly after a gutsy new monarch acceded. Apparently designed to be eaten right through, it ran: turbot *grillé*; kippers *au beurre*; *poulet grillé*; bacon; *oeufs cocottes*; *viande froide*; Scotch scones.

The Beeton-style breakfast was mounted in full splendour at Edwardian house parties, where guests, their appetites sharpened by adultery, lifted the silver helmets from long rows of chafing dishes and eagerly sniffed the kedgeree and friendly offals. It always made an agreeable scene in a play, as in Coward's *Hay Fever*, with its keenly awaited line, 'This haddock is disgusting.' There are still very grand hotels (see your *Good Hotel Guide*) where breakfast is served like this, with 15 kinds of marmalade and trolleys weighted with stewed prunes, rhubarb and gooseberries as well as 'segments'. And there are still regional variations. In Scotland, if haddock with poached egg fails to appeal, what about haggis? In Wales, why not try fried seaweed with your bacon?

The first foreigners to undermine the British breakfast were the food faddists of America's Mid-West, abetted by the Seventh Day Adventists of Battle Creek, Michigan. Between them, they invented new things to do with grain: shredding, flaking and puffing it from guns. In so doing they found how to extract the highest possible profit from a single grain of wheat. Quite early this century the British breakfast began to go snap, crackle, pop. Many mothers held out against the RTE (ready-to-eat) revolution, contending that porridge, laboriously made the night before, was the ideal lining for a child's stomach, especially if laced with treacle. The Scots – well, some of them – had a disgusting habit of making a week's supply of porridge and keeping it in a drawer, to be hewn out as required. Children abominated lumpy porridge; besides, you never got free gifts with it.

Gradually the middle-class breakfast came down to cereals, bacon and eggs, toast and marmalade. The admirable ladies who, between the world wars, provided cyclists with bed and breakfast for five shillings always served spanking breakfasts of this type (their successors still do, while swearing they are bankrupting themselves). The Great British Breakfast of five or six courses was now to be found increasingly in hotels; or, most prodigally, in ships at sea.

I still have a menu dated May 1, 1935 setting out the breakfast fare in Tourist Class aboard RMS *Antonia*, a small and sluggish Cunarder on the Atlantic run. It began with compote of prunes or figs, baked apple, grapefruit, orange juice, honeydew melon and bananas; proceeded to porridge and eight cereals, including grape nuts and post toasties; continued with fried whiting and Yarmouth bloater: thence to bacon (Canadian, Wiltshire or Danish) and grilled ham

(Cumberland and Canadian) and eggs in every style; and so, rather oddly, to Scots collops with mashed potatoes. That was only the hot menu; there was a cold buffet of roast mutton, brawn, pressed beef and galantine, with Spring onions. Hot or cold, the viands were washed down with tea (Indian, Ceylon or China), coffee, cocoa, chocolate or malted milk (plain or chocolate).

This, let it be clear, was merely the Tourist menu. Up in First they consumed steaks and chops like Japanese wrestlers. It was essential to keep yourself going until 11 am, when there would be sandwiches and soup, with a six-course luncheon at one. Compare these morning riches with the miserable breakfasts in a Jumbo jet. Compare them with the dastardly do-it-yourself pig-it-in-the-bedroom breakfast (a couple of 'croissants' in a bag and brew your own tea) in your friendly airport hotel.

The rage for travel also helped to undermine the Great British Breakfast. Many itinerant Britons, against their better judgement, decided that fresh French bread, genuine croissants and decent coffee made not a bad start to the day, despite those despicably thin flat packets of butter and *confiture* (few fancied the alternative French breakfast of coffee, cognac and half a camembert). Unfortunately, no decent French bread was to be had in Britain, or if it was, nobody could be bothered fetching it; but the waverers tried breakfasting on toast and coffee and found that, oddly enough, they did not miss bacon and eggs. Many admired the Dutch breakfast, with cold meat, cheese and eggs, but thought it perhaps too like high tea. The Russian breakfast proved to be a poor Dutch breakfast; unless, like some of the comrades, you ordered caviare with brandy.

Some holidaymakers came home talking of the joys of breakfast under a sun umbrella on a Mediterranean beach, not bothering to mention that the crisp rolls were in fact stale,

sweetish cakes and that the gleaming coffee jug contained hot water which was ceremoniously poured into a cup containing Cafe Nes. Others prattled about the sensual Jamaican breakfast, where you sat among the humming birds on your private balcony above your private cliff, and your private maid brought a basket with six kinds of tropical fruit, followed by – what a surprise, bacon and eggs.

Now people are pretending to rave about the Israeli breakfast, a singularly un-English and cucumber-haunted meal consisting of white pastes, mushes, endless salads, yoghourt, sour milk, cold fish and something called hummus, 'the Israeli breakfast of champions'. This meal, they tell you, had its origins in the kibbutz where people work for hours before they do any serious eating. An un-English meal, yes; but the yoghourt at least is catching on.

Britons streaming to America to save money may well come back clamouring for waffles, pancakes, buckwheat cakes and muffins (English, blueberry, apple, currant – you name it), all with maple syrup. Just conceivably, they may fall for hominy grits. They may even start doing those odd things Americans sometimes do with meat and jam. The American breakfast seems to vary round the world; in a Tokyo hotel it may consist of hot beef stew, fried potatoes and carrots. It would not surprise me if America ended up as the last home of the Great British Breakfast.

May 1980

Anon.

THE CRIMES OF EATING

Sir Robert Peel and her Majesty's Ministers have, we learn, taken a hint in criminal jurisprudence from his Worship the Mayor of Reading, and are now preparing a bill for Parliament, which they trust will be the means of checking the alarming desire for food which has begun to spread amongst the poorer classes of society. The crime of eating has latterly been indulged in to such an immoderate extent by the operatives of Yorkshire and the other manufacturing districts, that we do not wonder at our sagacious Premier adopting strong measures to suppress the unnatural and increasing appetites of the people.

Taking up the sound judicial views of the great functionary above alluded to, who committed Bernard Cavanagh, the fasting man, to prison for smelling at a saveloy and a slice of ham, Sir Robert has laid down a graduated – we mean a *sliding – scale* of penalties for the crime of eating, proportioning, with the most delicate skill, the exact amount of the punishment to the enormity of the offence. By his profound wisdom he has discovered that the great increase of crime in these countries is entirely attributable to over-feeding the multitude. Like the worthy Mr Bumble, in *Oliver Twist*, he protests 'it is meat and not madness' that ails the people. He can even trace the origin of every felony to the particular kind of food in which the felon has indulged. He detects incipient incendiarism in eggs and fried bacon – homicide in an Irish stew – robbery and house-breaking in a basin of mutton-broth – and an aggravated assault in a pork sausage. Upon this noble and statesmanlike theory Sir Robert has based a bill which, when it becomes the law of the land, will, we feel assured, tend effectually to keep the rebellious stomachs of the people in a state of wholesome depletion. And as we now punish those offenders who break the Queen's peace, we shall, in like manner, then inflict the law upon the hungry scoundrels who dare to break the Queen's Fast.

We have been enabled, through a private source, to obtain the following authentic copy of Sir Robert's scale of the offences under the intended Act, with the penalty attached to each, viz.:—

For penny rolls or busters	Imprisonment not exceeding a week.
For bread of any kind, with cheese or butter	Imprisonment for a month.
For saveloys, German sausages, and Black puddings	One month's imprisonment, with hard labour.
For a slice of ham, bacon, or meat of any kind	Imprisonment for three months, and exercise on the treadmill.
For a hearty dinner on beef and pudding	Transportation for seven years.
For do. with a pot of home-brewed ale.	Transportation for life.

As these offences apply only to those who have no right to eat, the wealthy and respectable portion of society need be under no apprehension that they will be exposed to any inconvenience by the operation of the new law.

1841

Anna Raeburn

LE COQ AU POT

My husband is a wonderful cook. I used to say this with pride but now admit it rather more ruefully because the trouble with his cooking is that I can't so much as cross the kitchen floor. It disturbs his *wa*, his harmony. You think I'm joking? It has reached the stage of the 'I'll just take these knives and then I'll go' routine. Not for nothing is the head of a kitchen called the chef – the chief, the big cheese: delicious but indigestible and assertive.

Few men are just all right cooks. They are either the 'not interested, women's work really' variety or the Escoffier special. There are those who will say deprecatingly that they can only whip up an omelette but then they tend to specialise in omelette whipping, even to the extent of giving parties serving nothing but omelettes with different fillings, or making a catering business out of their talents. There are women who don't cook but they tend either not to know that they can't or else to make a virtue out of the fact. A woman who can't cook is often a genius at something else, so excellent at whatever it is that the fact that she always eats out, or has somebody else to cook in, is taken as part and parcel of her achievement.

The thing is, women are supposed to cook. Men have choice in the matter. If women cook, it is generally, because of domestic

'To be honest, after a couple of weeks I'm quite happy to see him go back to his ship.'

expediency, every day. If men cook, it is as a hallmark of their broadmindedness, emancipation, imagination and creativity.

So, of course, they don't cook mince and tatties. They COOK. The price for this is unnecessary poundage and the introduction of a tactful note in the voice. After all, something of the order of quails in chocolate sauce cannot go unremarked. And if you are presented with such a dish by a man, it just isn't enough to say, 'Very nice, dear' and go on eating – which is what he very well might do were the situation reversed. The phrase is too obvious and the sort of conversational cliché which starts those awful man/woman confrontations over nothing, ie:

He: How is it?
She: Very nice dear.
He: What's the matter with it?
She: Nothing, it's very nice.
He: You think it's overseasoned?
She: Well – no. No. I like spicy food.
He: I should have stepped up the lemon.
She: I thought you used lime.
He: No, that was last time. I used grenadine and fresh lemon juice this time.
She: It's very nice.
He: You mean you preferred the lime?

and so on. This can be kept up *ad infinitum* depending on the stamina and/or bloody-mindedness of the people concerned.

There are those rare and wonderful couples who share everything in the way of responsibilities, so that he cooks one night and she another. They usually take it in turns to wash up and even shop on alternate days as well. But men and women who have so far broken the mould of culinary stereotyping are very rarely other than simple to the point of monastic about their food. It is true that they prepare food. It is less true to say that they cook.

And even in the case of men who cook frequently, most cannot approach the event without a build-up which suggests that simple appreciation will not be enough. First

of all, men who are going to cook fall into three groups:

(1) those who are going to ask you to do the shopping because they hate it,

(2) those who ask you to do most of the shopping but then rush off at the last minute to a particular shop for some unheard of condiment or seasoning without which, they imply, your efforts to provide the raw materials would have been as nothing, and

(3) those who insist on doing it all themselves and respond very irritably to the notion that four chicken breasts are still four chicken breasts, no matter who purchases them.

The trouble is that men become addicted to one magical ingredient and tend to add it to everything, then spend their time and

*'No, I haven't actually eaten ecrevisses à la bordelaise, but I **loved** the recipe.'*

'I'm sick to death of rabbit stew!'

energy counteracting the effect of the afore-mentioned talisman in the bubble-and-squeak. As a family we have so far survived a heavy commitment to allspice and hoisin sauce. It could have been worse. We have a friend who put tarragon in the Christmas pudding.

Then, while nobody likes making mistakes and falling short, men who cook are quite frightening if anything goes wrong. There have been occasions, to which I have been witness, where the language given vent to over a boiled egg could well have fried the damned thing. And although it is well known that the simpler things are often the hardest to do in the kitchen – like toasting bread or mopping up – there's not much pleasure left in them when they occasion such aggression.

Perhaps it is because they have to cook with such expected regularity that women become somehow desensitised to falling short. Unless she hasn't got anything better to worry about, a less than perfect Yorkshire pudding is just that, while, for a man, the same incident is the exposure of the vulnerability of his ego, and worse, the one that got away. Cooking is something still occasionally beyond man's control.

Men are very variable in their acceptance of the standards of food. When they meet together, away from women, no matter how highminded the purpose, they will accept food ranging from the agreeable if mediocre to the frankly grisly. The explanation given, should you be brave enough to draw attention to it, is that it's hard to get help these days, or it's a pity you had to come on an off-day because the food here is usually jolly good, or it's difficult to get a regular block booking anywhere and anyway most of us don't come here to eat! (this last accompanied by a knowing nod and a wink). The difference between what men will eat out and what they demand has always fascinated me, just as has the difference between what men will eat when they cook it and what they can't eat when somebody else does.

Yet everything a man does in the kitchen, a woman could do too, if she could be bothered. Which leads us to the conclusion that either men are much more insecure than women which is why they make such a fuss or, less fashionably, that they were brought up to be egocentric and demand praise for their every effort, especially if it is above and beyond what they consider usual.

As so often in matters gastronomic, the last word goes to the French: *la poule au pot, le coq au vin.* Even the carcass makes more fuss.

April 1987

'You'll regret this – I'm a renowned after-dinner speaker.'

ENTERTAINMENTS AT WHICH WE HAVE NEVER ASSISTED
A SMALL SECTION OF THE ANNUAL DINNER OF THE SOCIETY OF PUBLIC
ANALYSTS

Miles Kington

ATTENTION ALL WINE DRINKERS

10,000,000 gallons of adulterated wine were seized in Italy by the police last year. Among other things it contained bananas, dates, beet, peroxide, and chloroform. So, to bring your wine guide up to date, cut out this supplement and stick it in.

Banana: a kind of long yellow grape grown in Tuscany. Italian banana wine should be chilled and served with a dessert such as fruit salad or rice pudding. Green banana wine is sometimes found, though this has usually been adulterated with grass.

Beet: a kind of purple grape grown in Calabria. Not unlike good vintage turpentine, beet wine should be decanted at room temperature for two hours and then thrown away.

Bouquet: a small fragrant bunch of flowers often found in herbaceous wine.

Chloroform: an ordinary Italian wine, for which miraculous medicinal qualities are occasionally claimed.

Corked: term used of a wine made from cork.

Date: a kind of brown grape grown in small boxes. Date wine often has amusing small stones in it; more rarely, plastic forks.

Grape: a kind of green gooseberry without hairs, used formerly for making wine.

Gull's Egg Wine: fancy name given to wine made from old omelettes.

Ink: any red wine.

Madre di Santa Nicola: one of the great cauliflower wines of the world.

Mushroom: a kind of grey grape grown in caves. Not to be confused with toadstool wine.

Peroxide: a kind of blonde grape grown by shampooing ordinary grapes.

Raffia: an illegal Italian crime ring which makes wine out of old table mats.

Straw: the main ingredient of Chianti wine.

Table wine: wine made from tables.

Windfall: odd object added to apple wine.

February 1971

Fay Maschler

ONE POTATO . . .

I'm amazed, moved even, by how cheap some food is. When you think of the toil of sowing seed potatoes, growing them, digging them out of the ground, bundling them up, sending them off to markets, from where they are brought to shops and us, it is astonishing that they cost about 7 or 8p a pound.

I realise it isn't a currently held view that food is cheap but if you are in a position to restructure your way of eating, i.e. not having to satisfy a demanding mate or a bunch of children, it would be possible to eat delightful meals for very little financial outlay.

I'm not suggesting you grub around making salads from the dandelions Mother Nature sends up for free, I mean using what you can buy cheaply in shops and *concentrating* on it. It is not necessary, for instance, that potatoes should be an accompaniment. They can be a star performer, a soloist. If it is a suitable variety (and that is worth sorting out) you can rub a potato with a bit of oil and salt and bake it. A baked potato is a nice meal and, if you eat little else, not even particularly fattening. Lamb's kidneys, which can be bought cheaply, are good wrapped in a slice of bacon and then tucked into a hollowed out half-baked baked potato and the whole thing cooked for a further hour. The juices from the kidney soak into the spud. Mmmm.

Dumplings are another good way of handling potatoes. You could call them gnocchi if you were so inclined. Into about 1 lb of well beaten mashed potatoes mix 2 egg yolks, some herbs, salt and pepper, a grating of nutmeg or mace, and 1 heaped tablespoon fresh white breadcrumbs. Beat the two egg whites until stiff and fold them skilfully into the mash. Bring a large pan of salted water to the boil and drop in the mixture a dessert-spoonful at a time. Cover and simmer for about 10 minutes when the dumplings should have risen to the top and be cooked through. Scoop out with a slotted spoon and drain. They are good with melted butter and perhaps a sprinkling of Parmesan or sharp Cheddar cheese.

Chick peas are a commodity to consider. If every foodstuff has a drawback then chick peas' is that they have to be soaked overnight, which means that you must plan ahead. Once soaked, they are boiled in unsalted water for an hour or so until tender. One of the many advantages of this pulse is that they never go mushy, even if you leave them to boil much longer than necessary. Having cooked them, you might make Hoummous. Save the cooking liquid from, say, $\frac{1}{2}$ lb of chick peas. Crush the peas in a large plastic bag with a rolling pin (this gives a nice nubbly texture) or liquidise with some of the cooking water. When they are pulverised, thin down with a little more of the cooking water and then add $\frac{1}{4}$ pint of Tahina paste which is made from sesame seeds and can be bought from Cypriot grocers and health food stores, the juice of two lemons, two crushed garlic cloves and salt. Taste it and see if you want to adjust any of the flavours. Pile it into a shallow dish and dribble a little olive oil on top; very good eaten with hot bread and raw onion.

Another means of ingesting these cheap chick peas is to mix them with spinach as follows, a recipe taken from the suitably titled *Poor Cook* by Susan Campbell and Caroline Conran. Cook $\frac{1}{2}$ lb chick peas as described above. Fry a slice of white bread in olive oil. Put aside. Fry a chopped onion in the oil remaining, then add 3 tomatoes peeled and chopped. Wash 1 lb of spinach, shake it and sprinkle it with salt. Heat two tablespoons oil in a large pan, add 1 table-spoon paprika and stir it in. Add the spinach and when it is lightly fried put the mixture into a saucepan with the chick peas, onions and tomatoes. Pound a clove of garlic, add the fried bread and pound some more. Add this mixture to the chick peas and spinach. Cover and simmer for half an hour, when you will have a fragrant vegetable stew, thickened and interestingly flavoured by the pounded fried bread, and you will have the satisfaction of having made a nourishing and sustaining dish.

There are some foods that would surely be more prized if they were more costly.

'Not the curried beef again!'

Mussels are an example. There they lie in great vats at your local fishmonger (should you be so lucky as to have a local fishmonger and one that bothers to bring in mussels) looking as if they've just been picked up off a beach, as indeed they have, and costing only about 40p a pound.

I feel some people are put off mussels on the grounds that they must be tedious to clean or the belief that a bad mussel will slip undetected into the soup and *do you in*.

Firstly, apart from giving them a good wash to remove mud and loose grit and pulling off the straggly 'beard' that hangs from the hinge of the shell, they need no more serious cleaning, and the ones that are dead make it perfectly obvious by gaping wide open and refusing to close when tapped or shaken or spoken sharply to.

To cook them, you put a little water, or wine, or cider in the bottom of a large pan, pile in the mussels, cover and bring the liquid to the boil, shake the pan around and after a few minutes they are opened up and ready. The 'stock' in the pan can be strained through a wrung-out tea towel or piece of muslin laid in a sieve and made into a sauce with egg yolks and cream, or a *roux* or just cream. Alternatively you can pull off one half of each mussel shell (the half the mussel isn't nestling in) and onto each mussel put a dab of butter flavoured with crushed garlic and finely chopped parsley. Place the mussels in a shallow, fireproof dish and put under the grill till the butter is melted and bubbling. Eat with brown bread to mop up the sauce; a similar principle but actually better, more recognisable, than snails. Food is cheap if you stop thinking that you must have meat, potatoes and veg at every meal. You needn't. You might even start tasting each thing in its own right. Try it.

February 1979

Cyril Taylor

CHERRIES

I'm glad the cherry season's over.
I might have done a dash-and-grab
From a taxi-cab,
Assaulted a fruiterer or smacked
A greengroceress – run amuck, in fact.
But let me explain.
When cherries appear things happen in my
   brain.
Ever since I was that high
I've had a fat eye
For a cherry. With the lightest of light hearts
I'd rob a poor-box for a pound of white-
   hearts.
Strange – because I don't give a hoot

For most fruit.
I'm not a man that gapes
Voluptuously at hot-house grapes,
Or ogles the out-of-reach
Velvety-skinned peach.
Nor am I one that absorbs
Great quantities of rasps and strawbs,
Or succumbs
To the purple lure of plums;
And if ever I'm among felons
It won't be for stealing melons –
It will be cherries.
Not the sort with a high blood-pressure,
Ruddy and swarthy, but the fresher,
Paler, delicately-tinted beauties.
They are the cuties
I fall for – leave me a dish of these, two
   dishes, all that you've got,
And a little hummock of stones will mark the
   spot.
(But there's a snag,
Eating them as dessert. I like them out of a
   bag,
In the open. I don't wish to boast,
But I still spit a pretty stone, and farther
   than most.)
When cherries are ripe
I envy not the opium-fiend his pipe,
The bibber of wine
His anodyne;
The dreams that dwell in cherries are infin-
   itely sweeter;
I admit it – *I'm a secret white-heart eater.*

I'm glad the season's over.
To stop
In front of a shop
And see them there, all glossy and seductive,
Was painful (if instructive).
So dear and yet so far!
So wantonly, Wooltonly dear – that was the
   jar.
It wasn't easy, having to walk around
Resisting cherries – at four bob a pound.

August 1941

Jonathan Sale

THE SOUND OF MUESLI

If you are what you eat, I am 45 milli-grammes of Powdered Motherwort, 45 mg of Kelp, the best bits of 90 mg of Mistletoe, 45 kg of Scullcap, the same again of Wild Lettuce and a host of other herbal goodies, that make up Sunerven. This is said to be 'for irritability, nervous debility, sleep-lessness and nervous dyspepsia', although clinical tests carried out on my own nervous system have not produced a scientifically noticeable improvement on my temper. The worst that can be said of it is that it contains well below the lethal dose of Powdered Motherwort and is thus harmless, which is more than can be claimed for what comes out of conventional medical laboratories. Make the most of those claims about irri-tability and sleeplessness; under forth-coming regulations, the label will probably say something like 'This is a traditional remedy to calm you down, but if you get really jittery, consult your GP.'

Despite its claims to be 'The Herbal Tran-quilliser', Sunerven is at the steamed-up end of the health food business. Any health food shop will have shelf upon shelf laden with 'natural' products that, while not exactly promising the secret of Eternal Youth or of turning base metals into gold, suggest they can deliver rather more than most scientists could verify in their test-tubes. All of this is much to the annoyance of conventional medical merchandisers, who must, after dis-asters like Thalidomide, conduct test after test before marketing the mildest headache remedy.

If you are what you eat, I am 200 mg of Vitamin C Naturtabs (containing honey and natural lemon oil) and another 200 mg of Top C (Vitamin C with rose hips and acerola cherry). Ironically enough, as I sat down to write about health foods, I was struck by my worst cold for a year, and, following the advice of *Natural Cold Cures* by Maurice Hanssen and Jack Eden, turned to Naturtabs and Top C. Since these cost 60p and 70p for 50 tablets, and since 62p will purchase 100 similar dosage Vitamin C tablets from Boots, cynics with streaming noses might be prompted to ask if honey and rose hips make for real value at twice the price. Health food products have a turnover of £40 million a year, and cynics with wet handkerchiefs understand why.

By this point in my argument, purveyors of Powdered Motherwort will be hinting darkly that *Punch* is clearly in the pay of the big food and drugs manufacturers. If that allegation is true, those manufacturers are not getting their money's-worth, since it is time to turn a jaundiced and streaming eye on the big business of food.

According to a recent report, *Changing Food Habits in the UK*, we are eating badly and even dangerously. Three-quarters of all food in Britain is now processed at least once, and what has been added and subtracted makes most of the stuff on our plates a far cry from anything growing or grazing on the earth. As the trend towards richer, sweeter, softer and more monkeyed-about foods con-tinues, a smaller number of large manu-facturers dominate more and more of the market.

Bread is the Number One Exhibit in any Rogues' Gallery of British Noshing. Three companies have sown up 70 per cent of the market, and most of what they produce is white and anaemic. To call white bread Plas-ticine or sawdust is, according to wholemeal fans, an insult to the nutritional values of Plasticine and the vitamin content of sawdust. By the time the bread has been refined, robbed of some of its vitamins, given a few of them back, sliced and packaged, it may sell better and last longer on the shelf, but will give terrible value. By this it is meant that the loss of fibre in the refining process has been linked with appendicitis, bowel cancer, varicose veins and other ailments which might not occur if fibre was available from this and other sources, such as breakfast cereals – and it is not available, since refinement has crept in here too. No wonder that a Campaign for Real Bread has been formed. It is, alas, up against a lot of dough; the bread industry has a turnover of £450 millions, representing in this one product more than ten times the entire business of all health food merchandisers.

Much the same case can be made out against other foods that slip down the British gullet. As Western man and woman put more on their plate, they are getting less out of it. We are on the American road, of which Dr Curtis Wood, author of controversial *Overfed But Undernourished*, says: 'Your domestic pets may be getting more nutritive value from their food than you and your family get from yours.' The same could be true where people have taken to buying bran from pet shops (not recommended by Maurice Hanssen, who when not writing books on colds and other matters is President of the Health Food Manufacturers' Association, since pet shop bran could easily contain non-health food rat droppings).

What should be done by anyone who doesn't want to pop off just yet from a bad attack of bad food? Fresh vegetables and fruit seem to be half the battle, but they must be free of sprays and must have been grown without artificial fertilisers, which are said by health food enthusiasts to be bad for soil, plant and human alike. Is this enough? It is not, according to Barbara Cartland.

Barbara Cartland is one of the school that holds to the theory of 'supplements',

additions to the normal diet. She takes 80 pills a day, and enthused to me over her Stress Pill, her Brain Pill, and something known as RNA, which is very expensive and which peps up the cells to provide vitality so that one is able 'to look better and to be stimulated in all one's physical activities'. She says, 'It works, it works! The proof of the pudding is the brain – and that's me!' She is certainly conscious of her youthful looks. The Corgi production team responsible for *Barbara Cartland's Book of Useless Information* were so fed up with her corrections to the colour proof of her portrait on the cover that they only satisfied her by

'I'd like a hard sell if you could manage one.'

sending back a version which had not gone through the black plate, and the published version, out this week, is remarkably free of the wrinkles to be expected from a lady whose first novel was published in 1923. She certainly works at a frenetic pace, answering letters that arrive at the rate of sackloads a day, dictating 8,000 words of her next book in an afternoon. 'If I give up my pills, I shan't be able to write,' she says, and if there exists in any reader's mind the coarse and obvious rejoinder, well, he is no gentleman. 'I'm interviewing servants on top of it – it's all enough to kill a normal person.'

She endorses products by the barrel-load, but receives no money from manufacturers. 'They do pay for my postage and they help a bit with my secretary.' Anyone writing –

and how they do write, 6,000 people inquiring after one product she mentioned on one radio show! – receives a handful of appropriate leaflets. To me she sent a sample packet of Gev-E-Tabs ('All the vitamins and minerals you need'), two Stress Pills, a couple of Vitamin E capsules (for 'loss of sexual and general vigour' – thank you, Miss Cartland), samples of Super Korean Ginseng ('reputed by the Chinese to be of great value in preserving strength, vigour and vitality', any complaints to the Chinese, please) and three lozenges made from Propolis (produced by bees, defends human health, as recommended by Herodotus the Greek, wonderful for colds). I also received a handy checklist of which vitamin deficiency causes which condition.

Barbara Cartland's critics say that *all* her wonder cures cannot be the ultimate saviour of mankind; her widespread enthusiasms go over the top. Many scientists dispute the value of vitamins taken in massive doses; the only vitamin C you need, for example, is enough to keep scurvy at bay, and since not many of us are cooped up on nineteenth-century sailing ships, we don't have much need of it. But since she receives such a quantity of postage from those not highly educated in medical science and bothered about some part of their physical well-being, she clearly fulfils a need not met by the National Health Service.

The health food business is a reflection of the current awareness that we are not as flourishing as we might be, and is part of the movement that ranges from a little gentle jogging to the members of the International Association on the Artificial Prolongation of the Human Lifespan. As always, big business follows the fads, and sometimes dilutes the virtues it seems to offer.

To return to bread. A *Which?* survey by Julian Edwards discovered that people who thought they were buying, and indeed selling, wholemeal bread, were in fact handling so-called 'wheatmeal', which could have as much as 20 per cent of white flour. In some instances the brownness of the flour was due to the original flour being refined and whitened, and then dyed brown again with caramel colouring.

Another one to watch for is the best-selling of the Swiss-style breakfast cereals, Alpen. Although not considered as part of the health food trade, it is sold in health food shops, for 35p a 12 oz pack. For one thing, it can be bought at Tesco for 28½p. For another, Tesco do their own Swiss-style cereal at a mere 19½p. Ah, but that can't be so good, Alpen could retort. Ah, health food freaks retort, Alpen isn't that good either. Fruits, considered an essential part of muesli, are represented here by a scattering of sultanas or raisins. Worse, the third greatest constituent in order of weight is that star of two influential books, *The Saccharine Disease* and *Pure, White and Deadly*, refined sugar. I won't go into the arguments about the overloading of the pancreas, and must state that they are not universally accepted. What matters is that he who thinks he is following the health food party line by eating the (very tasty and appealing, partly thanks to the sugar) Alpen plateful, has misled himself.

There is nothing wrong with making money out of real wholemeal foods, of course, and the more there is of this the better. If Sainsbury's thought they weren't showing a profit in their wholemeal bread, they would pack it in, and my breakfasts would be that much poorer. It is only by the big manufacturers cashing in – wholeheartedly – on the health food interest that organically grown produce will be widely available.

Much the same is true of the patent medicines. Because of what Jill Wordsworth, author of *Diet Revolution*, refers to as 'orthodox medicine's concern with disease rather than health', people as concerned with their bodies as they are with their cars feel tempted to strike out in bizarre directions of their own.

What we need is an end to health food shops. They should be allowed to wither away, in the face of their ideas being stolen by big food stores and medical scientists, who could sort out the useful from the useless, instead of leaving it to the unqualified and the gullible. If Powdered Motherwort turned out to be an efficacious remedy, it should be on every prescription form. If not, any outstanding supplies should be tipped into the nearest pond. Nature works in a wonderful way and – who knows – it might improve the temper of the frogs. At any rate it, or the rose-hips, cured my cold.

November 1977

'An excellent meal. My compliments
to the gardener.'

Cyril Ray

FIZZ AND FROLIC

Champagne came late into the world of wine. No bubbly bubbled, no fizz fizzed, for the bibbers of bygone days: it was some sort of still stuff with which Omar the tent-maker bade his Belovèd fill the cup that cheers, and she seems to have done so fairly frequently, for him to exclaim:

Drink! for you know not whence you came,
nor why;
Drink! for you know not why you go nor
where ...

(I know the feeling) – and Noah the boat-builder, who began to be an husbandman and he planted a vineyard; and he drank of the wine, and was drunken, must have got into that sorry state of half-seas over, known to many a sailor come ashore, without benefit of the secondary fermentation in bottle that brings the beaded bubble winking to the brim.

All this I am sure of, for the tendency of young wine to resume a winter-retarded fermentation in the spring after the vintage is known only in such cool climates as that of

Champagne, and Omar's Persia and Noah's Near East are both rather on the warm side.

What is more, the secondary fermentation has to be both encouraged and controlled, and it was not (it is generally supposed) until Dom Pérignon became cellar-master of the Benedictine monastery at Hautvillers in 1668 and, according to Edward Hyams, went 'some way towards bringing the destructive demon of pressure in the bottle under some sort of control' that champagne became a manageable and, as a consequence, a marketable wine.

Dom Pérignon did not actually *invent* champagne – the secondary fermentation is a natural process, and it would seem that those people had already been enjoying the sparkling young wine who had happened to be in the right place at the right time. What Dom Pérignon achieved was to make it possible for it to reach the right tables.

It arrived very smartly at the very smartest tables of all. Louis XV, the Well-Beloved, came to the throne during Dom Pérignon's lifetime, and it was his own well-beloved Pompadour who proclaimed it to be the only wine that left a woman still beautiful after drinking it.

As beauty lies in the eye of the beholder, one might suppose that whoever was sharing her bottle must have told her so for, as Gavin Ewart has said,

A remarkable thing about wine,
which we drunkards and lechers all bless so,
is the way it makes girls look more fine
but ourselves, on the contrary, less so,

were it not that another sporting lady of the Well-Beloved's court, perhaps the lady who went in first wicket down, or maybe no more than a member of the second eleven, was more precise in observing that 'champagne gives brilliance to the eyes without flushing the face'.

I suppose that that's one thing in its favour. I have long since ceased to concern myself about the brilliance of my own or, indeed, anyone else's eyes: my personal endorsement of the life-enhancing fluid was

BANX

'Maybe you'd like something to drink, sir, before the mirage starts.'

expressed in the poignant lines of a debonair young poet, the Rupert Brooke of EC4:

I've tried, but it's always in vain,
<u>Not</u> to drink so much champagne,
But when I'm in trouble
I <u>do</u> need that bubble
– and it happens again and again . . .

Some say that it's because the bubbles carry the alcohol quickly into the bloodstream, but the very look of them bucks you up and, as John Jorrocks put it, 'champagne certainly gives one werry gentlemanly ideas' – a pity that he went on to qualify this irreproachable sentiment with, 'but for a continuance, I don't know but I should prefer mild hale.' All the same, he had the right idea about bubbles: it all happened in Paris at the Café of the same name, with his host's pouring him out a glass of still champagne, and Jorrocks 'holding it up to the candle: "*Garsoon! Garsoon!* – no good – no bon – no fizzay – no fizzay," giving the bottom of the bottle a slap with his hand to rouse it. "Oh, but this is still champagne," explained [his host] "and far the best". "I don't think so," retorted Mr Jorrocks, emptying the glass into his washstand.'

Quite right, too. Still champagne is all very well – I have enjoyed many a glass, and hope to enjoy many more – but there are plenty of places, from New Zealand's South Island to our own southern slopes, taking in Western Europe on the way, not to mention a sidle sideways, from California to Bulgaria, that make good still white wines, many of them at least as good as, and less expensive than, still champagne. But nowhere save in Champagne is the effervescent stuff made that is legally entitled to the name.

That effervescence is the cause not only of the fizz in the champagne itself, but it is conveyed by champagne into other potations – to wit, Black Velvet, which is compounded of Guinness and champagne, in equal amounts; Buck's Fizz, which ideally is made by mixing one part of freshly-squeezed orange-juice with two of champagne, both ice-cold; *champagne-cassis* (or *kir royale*), which is a teaspoonful of black-currant liqueur in a tall champagne tulip,

'Or there's a "Titanic Stopper", gin, brandy, vodka, lots of crushed
ice, dash of Angosturas, always goes down well in the warm
weather, or there again you can have . . .'

'Would you care to buy me a vodka and tonic? I hate drinking alone.'

topped up with fizz. The colour of which reminds me of pink champagne, which is not to be dismissed, as some folk have dismissed it, in the past, as frivolous. It is made seriously, and should be taken seriously, yet is nevertheless the wine *par excellence* for festivity and fun – and the prettiest.

I should add here, too, if it be that summer is near upon us, that the coolingest of drinks is well-chilled champagne with a bruised sprig of fresh mint in it, and that for frolicsome al frescos much is to be said for using sweet champagne instead of the recommended fizzy bottled lemonade in mixing your Pimm's, which then becomes a Pimm's Royal.

I have little in common with the late Maynard Keynes, save that he has been referred to (by the sainted Godfrey Smith of the *Sunday Times*) as the greatest Englishman of the century; that I cannot suppose he would have been able to abide Mrs T; and,

above all, the sentiment attributed to him in Roy Harrod's biography:

'... in his last two or three years he was in the habit of saying on festive occasions that the only thing he seriously regretted about the way in which he had managed his life was that he had not drunk more champagne ...'

It would be pleasant to have read, too, that on one or other such occasion the postprandial toast had been the one I found in the early-Victorian *The Toastmaster's Companion: Loyal, Patriotic, Naval, Military, Love, Bottle, Masonic, Sporting and other Toasts and Sentiments:*

Champaign to our real friends, and
Real pain to our sham friends.

July 1985

'Doctor, I get very depressed
in between breakfast,
lunch, tea and dinner.'

'OK if I don't bother about the twist? There's nobody here but us.'

'She'll never get the asking price. The place is riddled with sherbet.'

Colin Howard

UP FROM THE COUNTRY

'Why don't you come with me, one night?' said the grower.

'I don't know,' I said.

So I went.

'What have we got aboard?' I inquired, when he picked me up in his lorry outside my gate.

'Bunched carrots. They'll be the only bunched ones in the Garden to-night, you mark my words.'

(I marked them, and they were.)

'That all?' I said. At one time I was all for carrots, but I rather went off them when the facts about Radar got around.

'Sprouts,' he said. 'Twenty-seven boxes – twenty-eight pounds to a box.'

'How many plants to a box?'

'Let me see. Oh, about seven.'

I climbed up beside him, and we drove off.

'Nice to have a bit of company,' he said. 'I get a bit tired of doing this trip on my own three nights a week.'

'Is it cheaper to take them up in your own lorry than to send them by rail?'

'It is now.'

We were in Hampshire, it was seven-fifteen in the evening, and he said he wanted to be at Covent Garden by ten. As we were only just in Hampshire – in fact we had got into Surrey while we were talking – we had plenty of time to stop at a pub for a few games of darts. He whitewashed me twice, with consummate ease. There is that to be said for making the trip three times a week.

We rattled through Sunningdale and Egham into Staines, rumbled sedately through Ashford into the Great West Road – we had an uneasy feeling there was a porpoise-like police-car astern, and we were covenanted to thirty miles an hour – jolted through Brentford, and crawled humbly along Piccadilly to the Garden. It was twenty past ten as we pulled up outside a dead, shuttered warehouse.

'Too late!' I said despairingly.

'They don't start unloading till midnight,' he said.

'Then why,' I demanded with justifiable heat, 'drag me away before closing-time?'

'Because I want to get away again in decent time. The later you come the longer you have to wait to be unloaded.' He indicated a lorry parked in front. 'We're lucky. Only one ahead of us.'

The kerbs of the streets radiating from the Garden were lined with silently waiting lorries. We jumped out and went into a dive-ish sort of place for sausages-and-chips. Then we had a drink and went back to the lorry. We got inside the cab, turned up our overcoat collars and lay back and dozed. The rain drummed down on the roof and glittered off the road.

We were aroused by a rasping roar. The shutters were being run back, the warehouse was opening up. A yawning, tousle-headed youth emerged and sprinkled sawdust over the wet pavement. We climbed down and

stretched. We found we had seniority over four more lorries, tailing round the corner. The driver of the lorry ahead of us, a squat, muscular Londoner, looked up and down the unpeopled street and spat with a kind of impatient resignation.

'The day them outside porters is here on time,' he muttered, 'I'll sign the pledge.'

Three more yawning men appeared. These were inside men, employed by our wholesaler. One took a broom and swept out the premises, raising a fine mound of derelict fruit and vegetables. The others lined up on the threshold and stared across the pavement at us. We leaned on the lorry and stared back. Until the outside porters arrived it was stalemate.

'What would happen,' I asked the grower, 'if we unloaded your stuff ourselves?'

He went deathly pale.

'England would be without fresh vegetables for six months.'

'Would it be such an unpopular move as that?'

'Listen. I take the stuff off the lorry and pass it to the outside porter. The outside porter carries it across the pavement and hands it over to the inside staff. It is then all theirs. The fact that I could chuck my stuff from the lorry over the pavement and into the shop is beside the point. I am compelled to employ the link.'

'Even when it's a missing link?'

'Yes.'

'Are you serious about there being a strike if you got tired of waiting and did the job yourself?'

'Well, fairly. It's definitely advisable to wait. Anyhow, they get paid for every single lorry that comes into the Garden whether they've unloaded it or not. So, what with one thing and another, one just waits.'

The inside staff filled in time making ready for the buyers. They opened boxes of pears and tomatoes, dived their hands into barrels as though they were bran-tubs, fetching out

'Sorry about this, but our microwave is on the fritz.'

bunches of green grapes and blowing the granulated cork off them.

'What time do the buyers start coming?' I asked a man emptying a sack of carrots into a crate.

'Half-past five. Half an hour later in most other places.'

'Do you stop buying yourselves then?'

'Bless you, no. The lorries'll be delivering stuff till ten in the morning.'

He sorted carefully through the crate of carrots, putting aside some two dozen of the finest. He emptied the rest back into the sack, rolled down the top, and dressed it appetisingly with the hand-picked carrots. Then he started on a sack of onions.

At half-past twelve an outside – and outsize – porter arrived, a great, beefy fellow who hefted the sacks of swedes from the lorry ahead as though they were sacks of feathers.

'Makes fifteen to twenty pounds a week,' whispered the grower.

I instantly resolved to scratch my son from the school he was down for and enter him for Covent Garden instead.

The Garden was now wide awake. Lights blazed, engines throbbed, lorries rumbled through the narrow streets, snorting, reversing, swearing. A lorry, trying to pass between two others parked abreast, one each side of the road, failed, and a cataract of onions poured and bounced from a ripped sack. The lorry, backing and filling, passed over them, and we all gathered around and wept over them. The odour from a sackful of crushed onions is almost vocal.

At last it was our turn, and we clambered up on to our cargo. The grower straddled the carrots. I stood on the sprouts. We handed the boxes down to the porter, who received them into the sort of truck that (now I come to think of it) I haven't seen on a railway station for twenty years. For the last load, three cases of sprouts, he disdained the truck, and did it on his head. He had a thing like a rubber deck-tennis quoit inside the crown of his cap, but I should judge some of the weight must have got down to his neck as well.

One in the morning. The rain still coming down. The gutters and roadways carpeted with fresh vegetables. I don't know why anybody living in W.C.2 ever buys vegetables. All they have to do is to take a basket for a walk after midnight.

'Now for the empties,' said the grower as we put up the side board.

We drove round a couple of dark blustery corners, pulling up at a blacked-out warehouse in a forlorn little street. The iron gates to the yard were padlocked, and the grower said dash and bother it (or words to rather more than that effect), the old blank was out taking a stroll around the market as usual. We waited a dismal half-hour, and then the old blank, small and wizened, came pattering and snuffling through the lamp-lit rain. The old blank, the custodian of the empties to be brought back filled with produce next trip, grunted, which seemed to be his idea of 'Good evening,' and unlocked the gates. Within towered, half as high as the surrounding houses, monumental stacks of boxes (four bob on each). I thought what the Crazy Gang could have done there.

'I'm taking fifty-one, that's all,' said the grower.

The old blank grunted.

We located three barrows, picked out one with rubber tyres – only rubber-shod barrows allowed here at night – and piled the boxes into it. Up went a neighbouring window, with an angry rush.

'Hoy!' called a feminine voice, as Juliet might have called.

'Hoy!' returned the grower courteously.

'Turn it up, will ya?'

'Turn what up?'

'Cut out that row, or I'll call the cops.'

'Madam,' explained the grower, 'we're loading up.'

'Then you stop loading up!' advised the invisible lady.

'That,' said the grower, 'would be an impossible way to run a business.'

There was silence, possibly while the cops were contacted. We got our empties aboard. We exchanged farewell grunts with the old blank. It was ten-to-two as we drove off, took an arc of Piccadilly Circus, and set course for home.

'You'll be in bed quite early,' said the grower cheerily, as he dropped me at my gate at half-past three.

'I shall be,' I agreed, rubbing bleary eyes; 'for the next week.'

January 1951

Miles Kington

MAUVAIS APPETIT!

Now that a hygiene report has revealed that nine out of ten French restaurants are a health risk, keep this handy check-list beside you next time in Paris ...

Eating Out
SOME USEFUL PHRASES

Bonsoir. Je suis un inspecteur de santé publique et j'aimerais une table avec un lavabo.
Good evening. I am a public health inspector and I'd like a table with a wash-basin.

Garçon, il y a une mouche dans ma crème de bolets.
Waiter, there is a fly in my cream of Boletus mushroom soup.

Selon mon avis, ce jambonneau a contracté la peste porcine et je voudrais me faire rembourser.
In my opinion, this pig's knuckle has got swine fever and I'd like my money back.

Pourriez-vous échanger cette souricière qui ne fonctionne pas?
Could you change this unserviceable mousetrap?

J'ai mangé des cornichons / grives / myrtilles / bécasses / amourettes / brugnons et j'ai des vertiges.
I have eaten some gherkins / thrushes / bilberries / woodcock / spinal marrow / nectarines and I feel dizzy.

Envoyez-moi donc le maître d'hôtel, cette palourde est bouchée.
Fetch me the head waiter, this clam is blocked.

Malheureusement, j'ai trouvé des crottes dans mon croque-monsieur.
Unfortunately, I have found some droppings in my toasted ham and cheese sandwich.

Je voudrais quelque chose contre les brûlures d'estomac / la flatuosité / la dysenterie / l'hépatite / le trisme.
I'd like to take something for heartburn / flatulence / dysentery / hepatitis / lockjaw.

Où puis-je trouver une pompe stomacale?
Where can I find a stomach pump?

Quel est le voltage?
What is the voltage?

Je dois partir immédiatement.
You'll have to excuse me.

Eating Out
PASSAGES FOR TRANSLATION

Translate into French:

MR AND MRS DUPONT were seated in a grill-house beside an abattoir. They were swatting bluebottles and, from time to time, cuffing rodents as they scurried by. Since a quarter of an hour, they had been without a main course. Mr Dupont was becoming ill-humoured and Mrs Dupont was becoming indisposed from her starters. 'Attention there!' cried out Mr Dupont to the pastry chef who was idly mucking out a stove. 'Bring us a bucket and some Seltzer water and look sharp, there's a good fellow!' but the surly chap only spat contemptuously into a tureen and cleaned inside his ear on a napkin. At last, the Duponts could not shoulder it any longer. They took their leave in favour of a fashionable hotel on the corner of an avenue. There they lunched on beef-steak but it was, at it happened, tainted and they suffered foot and mouth disease. 'Next time,' avowed the Duponts, 'we shall stick to a long crusty loaf, some chocolate and a glass of ordinary wine!'

Translate into English
from *Phèdre A la Carte* by Egon Racine

PHEDRE: J'ai pris, j'ai fait couler dans mes brûlantes veines Un poisson, pris aujourd'hui de la Seine.

Déjà jusqu'à mon coeur la croquette parvenu
Dans ce coeur expirant jette un froid inconnu;
Déjà je ne vois plus qu'à travers un nuage
Et le ciel et le patron que ma présence outrage;
Et la mort, à mes yeux dérobant la clarté,
Rend au jour, qu'ils souillaient, toute sa pureté.

PANOPE: Elle expire, Seigneur!
LE PATRON: Si seulement je l'avais su!
Je préfère que le menu soit toujours bien entendu.

GLOSSARY

Cordon Sanitaire: Decoration awarded to sommeliers with clean fingernails.
Bain Marie: Staff washroom.
Rosette: Staff shower-room.
La Batterie de Cuisine: No mains electricity.
Spécialité de la Maison: Left-overs.
La Gastronomie: Study of Intestinal Infections.

Oliver Pritchett

SAINSBURY'S PEOPLE

In the evenings I like to browse through my collection of plastic carrier-bags. Here is a Tesco, blue-striped and in almost mint condition; and here is a Presto with its attractive pale yellow and blue squares. There is a small jagged tear in the side of it where the sharp corner of the Harvest Crunch cereal broke through. This is my Safeway with the broken handle caused by over-ambitious filling on my part – probably that extra bottle of Muscadet-of-the-month. And this is my trusty carrier-bag from Shepherd's supermarket; it served me well as a briefcase for a month or so.

Most poignant of all is this sensible stout paper bag from Sainsbury's. This does not just bring back memories of the celeriac, the salsify, the smoked eel and the impulsively-bought red mullet; it also reminds me of the Incident.

I remember I was in the poultry section, torn between a wild duck and a couple of partridges. My concentration must have lapsed for a moment, because I drove my trolley, not all that hard, into the ankle of a young woman who was wondering about guinea-fowl. Of course I said 'sorry', but my apology, which would have been readily accepted in Presto and say no more about it, was not good enough here. The woman denounced my carelessness, limped about rather theatrically, glared at me and made it quite plain that 'sorry' would not do in Sainsbury's. I had to go and cower by the croissants until she had finished her shopping and left.

They are a different class of customer in the posher Sainsbury supermarkets. They are the coarse-ground sea-salt type of people, unwise to rub up the wrong way. And they keep different hours. For example, at 9 a.m. on a Saturday morning in Safeway you could reckon to have the cold meats, pâtés and bean-sprouts salad section just about to yourself, but at this hour the Sainsbury's car-park is already absolutely full with dauntingly smart cars (silver green in colour) and you really have to jostle to get near the Jerusalem artichokes. Sainsbury's people make an early start so that they will be at their country cottages in time to de-frost the *moules farcies* before dinner.

*'I think food tastes so much nicer out of a
free-range supermarket trolley ...'*

I could not yet call myself a connoisseur, but I reckon I am an aficionado of super-markets. There used to be a lot of snobbery about them. People sneered about pre-pack-aged purchases, but nowadays the trend is towards de-packaging. You come out of the place with filthy hands after selecting your own potatoes one by one; your sweater is covered with flour after choosing the loaf baked on the premises; soon they will have gut-your-own herrings at the fish counter.

And, it goes without saying, the food is much more adventurous and exotic. If you want quails' knee-caps marinaded in sky-larks' tears, you are likely to find them on special offer at your local supermarket. They will probably be about five feet along the shelf from the crystallised rose-petal cocktail snax. Or you could take the alternative route past the pine kernels, turning left at the *cèpes*.

They used to say it was all brain-washing. A supermarket's middle-ranking executive Svengali, spying on you through one-way glass, could give you an irresistible urge to buy custard-powder simply by adjusting the piped music. He could position the stack of packets of sugar so that it ambushed you and forced you to buy. It adds a bit of spice to shopping: a chance to speculate about the philosophical question of free will. Did I really choose this boar's head pâté or did it choose me?

The most absurd thing they used to say about supermarket shopping was that it removed the human contact. The whole point of going to a supermarket is for the human contact – and not just with the oblig-ing girl who slices you the desired amount of Brie.

At my local store the human contact begins

at the door. You need a 10p coin to put in the slot to release a spare trolley from the chained-up herd. There is always a merry crowd of people at the door who, for a consideration, will let you have the trolley they have finished with.

I like all the etiquette involved: the way we smile when overtaking the woman with the decision-making crisis by the biscuits; the way we tut at the minority who go round anti-clockwise; the mass un-spoken disapproval of the man who parks his trolley in the check-out queue to save his place, then makes darting forays back to the shelves to pick up more items.

Then there are the social hazards. You are queuing to pay when suddenly you realise that it is the 'up to seven items' check-out. Do you ditch the muesli and the aubergine in order to qualify, or do you slink off to another queue?

Bateman could do a neat cartoon entitled: 'The woman who waited at the delicatessen counter for a quarter of Parma ham without first obtaining a numbered ticket.'

There are the mysteries of those Tannoy announcements. 'Mr Parker to check-out please,' they say. There is some secret life going on here. Are all the staff seething about the way Mr Parker, of soft cheeses, attacked Mr Willis, the tinned fruit supervisor, with a price-ticket gun over his love for the check-out cashier whose badge on the lapel of her crisp pink overall tells us that she is called Michelle? Is it a private code, to avoid mass panic in the store, to tell the staff that they are running dangerously low on pomegranates?

It is a pleasure to observe the other shoppers. You can tell that there are certain people who have a picture of the lay-out of the store in their minds and they have compiled their shopping-lists in the order that they will come to things as they make their progress round.

I like watching the couples. One of the pair, usually the one who steers the trolley,

is sensible and sticks to the list and concentrates on the basics. The other is subject to whims. The husband disappears from view and returns to the trolley with a mango, some radicchio and a pleased expectant expression. He is sternly sent off to put them back where they came from. A moment later he is back at the trolley pleading the case for a jar of anchovy-stuffed olives. The wife asserts her moral superiority with toilet-paper and lard.

Round by the pet food you will find families in earnest debate as to whether their dog would prefer jugged hare with extra marrow bone jelly or solid meaty chunks of venison.

From time to time I have absent-mindedly dropped one of my purchases into someone else's trolley. This can lead to interesting new friendships.

Mostly, however, I just like to see what other people are buying. It is pleasing that it is all so public. That woman, three yards in front, making her way down the beverages section, is putting on great airs, but she is betraying herself with the one hundredweight bag of frozen crinkle-cut chips, the fourteen cans of baked beans and the dozen frozen chicken dinners. There is a fellow showing off with a bucketful of yoghourt, some crispbread and a lettuce. Over there is a woman who belongs to that tiresome bulk-buying breed; she has clearly planned every single meal for the next three months and I certainly do not intend to get in the queue behind *her*. There, I knew it; she has just taken one of those eight-gallon bottles of fabric conditioner off the shelf.

Another woman is buying a gross of jars of pulped baby food and a gigantic carton of disposable nappies – enough to last her baby until it reaches the age of 27.

I like to try to avoid being summed up by the contents of my trolley and I try to throw the check-out voyeurs off the scent. Just as they are beginning to dismiss me as a cottage cheese and radishes type I chuck in a monster

'It's an unassuming little wine with a deceptively high veritas content.'

bag of salt'n'vinegar crisps and an economy pack of budgerigar cage liners. I will buy a pound of whitebait, then mystify everyone by making a bee-line for the spaghetti hoops.

Before you leave our supermarket there is one more pleasure and that is to admire the ranks of shopping-baskets on wheels which their owners have left by the door while they do their tour of the store. They are mostly box-like in shape and made of a sort of plastic fabric, I suppose, and all covered in various drab tartan patterns. What do these tartans signify? I like to believe they represent some of the great and famous names of the super-market world – the Clan Tesco, the Highland Branch of the Safeway, the Fighting Fine Fares, Presto of that Ilk and the Royal Sainsbury. Such evocative names, such a proud tradition.

July 1987

Roy Hattersley

BORN WITH A GREASY SPOON

Workmen's cafes are not just cafes where workmen go to eat. For workmen – like other members of the human race – differ in their capacity to make accurate judgments about price and value. Workmen eat in snack bars, pizza parlours, railway buffets and Italian restaurants. They consume beefburgers in garishly painted hangars which are especially constructed for speedy digestion. But although they may seek out places where the service is quick and the food on offer is

'Right! That's fifteen cod and chips, eleven chicken and chips and one fish cake on its own.'

convenient to consume, fast food and convenience catering is wholly incompatible with the menus which adorn workmen's cafe walls.

Workmen go to cafes looking for nutriment and they search for sustenance without thought of calories or carbohydrates. It is hernias not heart attacks about which workmen worry. By the end of the afternoon, they have worked off the lunch cholesterol and the blood is pumping happily through veins which have been unclogged by honest endeavour. Or, to put it another way, they can eat bacon and chips, or even bacon and chips with fried bread.

The workmen's cafe down the road from where I live advertises chips with half of the dishes which it offers on its hardboard menu.

But it is the smell of bacon which brings the customers in off the streets. To recall the words of Edith Cavell, chips alone are not enough. If they were, the Laughing Halibut on the opposite corner would not have turned into a betting-shop.

It is the bacon which pulls them in – bacon without the rind cut off, bacon that is miraculously fried so that it remains crisp whilst awash in hot fat and crinkles without shrinking to so small a shrivelled rasher that the customer demands two for the price of one. Naked bacon, lying flagrant on the plate, is, according to the cafe down the road, the most popular dish on offer. But it is bacon sandwiches which carry the real mark of workmen's cafe class.

The workmen's cafe bacon sandwich is, of

course, made out of sliced bread. The middle-class affectation of making sandwiches out of cobs, cottage loaves and batons is suitable only for Scandinavian fragments of salted fish and limp lettuce. In the privacy of one's own home, dipping the bread in the hot bacon fat is possible. For in the unhurried calm of domestic tranquillity, it is possible to lower the slice into the pan with a sensitivity which allows it to be coated with the liquid grease without impregnation to the point of sticky disintegration. Such niceties are not possible in the hurly-burly of the workmen's cafe.

The expedient which they have devised is brilliant. The two slices of bread – laid out like butterflies' wings in preparation to receive the bacon – receive a quick coating of warm margarine. The experienced cook/ waitress can cover each surface with a single stroke of her carving knife. Then, when the hot rashers are put into place, the whole viscous mélange coalesces into a single slab of laminated bliss.

I am ashamed to admit that down the road from me the workmen's cafe serves soft drinks. But I report with relief that it is the tea which swamps all other liquid sales. Tea still comes in thick cups (as is right) but is poured out with a delicacy which I find alien and offensive. The proper technique for tea preparation and pouring is well-established. It requires a large brown teapot, an urn of endlessly boiling water and a reckless willingness to pour away part of the product in order to ensure that only the very best of it is put on sale.

'Tea, please,' says the thirsty but polite customer. 'Mug or cup?' asks the attentive waitress. 'Mug,' comes back the profligate reply and the scene is set for a ritual as formalised as any that ever happens in a Geisha house. First, a sprinkling of new tea-leaves is added to those which have already seen long service at the bottom of the pot. Then the boiling water hisses out of the stainless

steel tap and whilst the tea mashes (they call it 'brews' down the road from me) the mug is placed on the stained, perforated metal grille which joins sink to counter. It is then that the special spell is cast. The mug *must* be filled to overflowing so that the brown nectar dribbles down its sides and disappears through the grille. Tea which can be carried in safety back to the table is not properly served.

Tea is the characteristic of the workmen's cafe which has survived in the inner suburbs of our great industrial cities. In the part of Birmingham which I know best the cafes are no longer Joe's but Imran's, Saeed's and Mohammed's. There tea is different. The milk is boiled with the water. And there is less enthusiasm for bacon sandwiches. But the spirit is the same. The orange chicken and the little Cornish pasties filled with gunpowder combine the virtues of modest price and high nutritional value which were exemplified by the fried eggs, baked beans and pure beef sausages which the previous owner served. They are also – like their indigenous predecessors – enormously friendly places in which to spend twenty minutes.

These days, too many workmen have no work to do. And the workmen's cafe down the road from me is a hundred yards away from the Salvation Army Hostel and almost opposite the Social Security office. I suspect that there are hours spent at its tables for nothing more than the price of a cup of tea and a piece of Bakewell tart. And as long as they do not consume food not purchased on the premises, nobody ever complains. Friendly anonymity is as typical of workmen's cafes as the bottles of brown sauce and the clogged-up salt pots. Life is better when washed down by a mug of tea – especially if it contains the magic spell that is cast by making it overflow.

July 1985

Larry

TRANSPORT CAFFS OF DELIGHT

'Another instance of the folly of not breastfeeding.'

Stanley Reynolds's
Good Jubilee Nosh Guide

TWENTY-FIVE YEARS OF SOUPE DU JOUR

'When I first came to the North of England, lad, before you were even a lad, lad,' I said to the lad, 'the only food they had in pubs were these sort of Scotch eggs in glass cases. They weren't there to eat. Just to look at.

Rather like something in the British Museum. At least I never saw anyone buy one and actually eat one. At least never twice. What'll you have?'

'I dunno,' he said, 'either the *boeuf à la bourguignonne* or the *coq au vin*.'

And this was at lunchtime. And in a pub. In the North of England. More than just the North of England. In Liverpool. We were in one of those old-fashioned cellar pubs, where you dive down below street level, and there is only just about elbow room. It is called the Corkscrew. We had just come from the Grapes, a tiny and very old pub, in Matthew Street, the fabled alley of the legendary Cavern Club which housed the famous Beatles, and where we had steak sandwiches, served very quickly. The barmaid gave us a piece of paper with a number written down and no sooner had she handed it to us than another barmaid was shouting our numbers out because our steak sandwiches were ready.

God, how things have changed in the last twenty-five years. I explained to the lad that in those days it was the union rule that wherever food was served in a pub in the North the management must employ the lame and the halt and the preferably stone-deaf whose function it was to growl 'Got none,' whenever anyone was stupid enough to ask for something to eat.

We were on a pub crawl, the lad and I. Not the boozy sort. But to check the food. Eating our way round the city to see how much things have changed in this Jubilee Year of Her Majesty the Queen as far as the English eating habits are concerned; and, also, perhaps, to try to see what will happen in the next quarter century of that most sovereign lady's rule. An unusual experience this, wandering from pub to pub eating rather than drinking. The drink in pubs has changed since the 1950s when I arrived from the old Massachusetts Bay colony. The ale is not as 'real' as it was then, but real ale is seeping back. And the pubs of the North are not dusty like they used to be. Plastic, yes. But clean plastic. And one can get a glass of wine nowadays.

'Lad,' I said, 'when our gracious lady first came upon the throne, if you walked into a pub and asked for a glass of wine, they all moved away from you. They thought anyone drinking wine would suddenly start foaming at the mouth. Now look at all the winos and plunkies in here guzzling the grape.'

'May I have a glass of wine, father?' the lad asked.

'Of course not,' I said, 'you start on that stuff you'll end up in the long grass down by the railroad tracks somewhere. Get a glass of milk. See, for the purposes of investigation, if the pubs of the North are as civilised as

the saloons of all the really old Wild West movies where Tom Mix and William S. Hart used to be able to buy a pint of milk.'

The change in drinking habits in the clean, well-lit plastic pubs of today has been written about at some length. The change in eating habits has been less well remarked. But it has been a startling change when you come to think about it, which is something I hadn't done much, my mind, oddly enough, usually being bent, like my elbow, to other work in a public house. The kid had the *boeuf à la bourguignonne*, which, he said, was all right but not like the real thing. Twenty-five years ago a sixteen-year-old would not have known what the real thing would have been like. Now he knows because we sometimes get those pre-frozen jobs at the supermarket; the supermarket which also sells all sorts of delicatessen food, mainly German and kosher, all signs of the changed times. I had the game pie. An old English thing, the game pie. Still in the 1950s, in a Northern pub, you wouldn't have been able to get one. And especially not an old English game pie handmade by Mustapha, the cook at the Corkscrew. Mr Ken Shipton, the large, nautically bearded manager of the Corkscrew, says his chef Mustapha, and the other Mustaphas and Frederics and Angelos, and the Tony the Greeks, are undoubtedly the reason why you can now get all sorts of European, Middle Eastern, and olde English grub in a public house today.

We couldn't get a pint of milk at the Corkscrew, however. 'We got none,' the lad was told. So at least some of the good old ways that have seen the Island race through dark times still hold true.

We staggered out and around the corner to the New Court Bar which was the local of the *Liverpool Post & Echo* where I used to work and which sometimes, in those days, would run to a cheese cob. Now a waitress came and we had the roast beef of old England and mash. At the Corkscrew I had

also had some of Mustapha's lemon chiffon pie. It was an uphill climb to a brand new place, Cafe-Kirkland's, which, I think, is a model of the way things will be when the Queen celebrates her half century. Cafe-Kirkland's is truly European. It is a real cafe, allowing families in. You can see babies there. You can also see – and this makes it a bit more than simply a European sort of cafe – plays. Just recently they've done a modern version of *The Good Soldier Schweik*, Bertold Brecht's *Senor Carrar's Rifles*; George Melly has been there; and a little thing of my own is being done at Cafe-Kirkland's as part of the Jubilee. These are at night. During the day, Mr Bernie Start, who is the sharpest dresser in Liverpool, has a string quartet playing downstairs – the musicians come from the Liverpool Philharmonic which is just up the road – and upstairs he provides a haven for street buskers. Kirkland's employs a doorman to salute the trade as they enter – not a bouncer,

mind, but a real doorman; another sign of changing times.

Although Kirkland's and, indeed, the Corkscrew and the other pubs we visited, may have some special Liverpool flavour about them, the food position in pubs is the same throughout the North now. Eating out at night might still be dodgy but lunchtime in pubs is a new world. The only bad change has been the death of seafood. But the same pollution, and over-fishing by Russian freezer ships, has killed the seafood bars of my native New England as well. And there is some hope in Manchester at least, when Sinclair's Oyster Bar, the famous fish house, built in 1354, opens again this year after being jacked-up and wheeled into hiding while Manchester's Old Shambles, the last of the old Tudor streets, was re-done by the city planners.

Foreigners coming to Britain, Britons going to foreign countries for holidays, has changed the eating habits. There are puzzlements, like my supermarket having a row of Mexican food, but this is quickly explained. The Mexican food is there because people go to Spain. A bit curious that. The answer is the Mexicans eat Spanish sort of food and they also have a bigger export industry, sending tinned food to the United States, and to Britain; to Spain, as well, Mr Howell, my supermarket owner, told me.

Mrs Sandy Hewson, who does the catering for Cafe-Kirkland's, says the only real conservatism she finds is that the British don't like eating with their hands. They had planned to have American style food at Kirkland's but where Americans will eat hamburgers, hot dogs, corn on the cob, chicken and God knows what – not in New England, my dear – with their hands, the English, even the Liverpudlian English, want a knife, fork and spoon. Fish and chips, she says, are the exception which proves the rule. 'We thought we'd just have snacks,' Sandy Hewson said, 'but we found people wanted more. Not with waiters pressing full course luncheons on them in an old-fashioned way. People don't want set sort of foods at set times any more. They want what they want when they want it.' Did she have such a thing as a glass of milk? No, they hadn't come that day.

And where did the future lie? What would it be like in twenty-five years' time?

'I think we'll go like the Americans,' Sandy said, 'and start eating with our fingers.'

'Yes,' the lad, a sceptic, said, 'and by that time the Americans will be eating with their feet.'

April 1977

Brian Murphy

PASS THE MALT

The most extraordinary whisky I ever tasted was served to me by an unkind BBC presenter on the *Nationwide* programme. It came out of a bottle shaped like an eagle, and the label claimed, if I remember correctly, that it was 'Extremely rare, fine, old selected pure malt whisky as distilled and bottled in the Highlands of Scotland. Made in Bombay'. It was such an amazing drink that I had to have another to make sure it had actually happened to me. As far as I could make out, it was a mixture of garlic, molasses and turpentine, and friends watching the programme told me later that my face was a study in conflicting emotions. They may well have been right.

However accurate that unforgettable label was, one thing was quite certain – the liquid behind it had never been within a hundred miles of malted barley. And malted barley is what single malt Scotch whisky is all about and what distinguishes it from all other whiskies and, indeed, from all other drinks. Briefly, malt whisky is the product of barley which has been soaked and allowed to germinate until all its starch has been converted to sugar, heated over a fire which contains peat, ground, mashed with hot water, the drained-off weak syrup fermented and then distilled in copper stills. Then aged in oak casks for at least five and usually many more years. Except, of course, for the large amount which is furtively shipped abroad to bolster up the whiskies of Bolivia, Ecuador, Tanzania and, for all I know, India. But we don't talk about that.

Blended whisky, on the other hand, is a mixture of a certain amount of malt – down to a fifth in some of the more unpalatable blends – and grain whisky, which is the product of a large-scale industrial process which produces large-scale quantities of a fairly flavourless alcohol which has to be casked and aged for at least three years. Then

'I'll have the executive martini and the businessman's lunch with a cup of corporate coffee.'

it can be blended with malt whisky to appear in the bottles of the familar and well advertised blends. I am not knocking blended whiskies. Some of them – like Black Label, for instance – are very fine whiskies indeed. It is just that they are not malt whiskies. And in my view any malt whisky – with one unmentionable exception – is better than any blended whisky.

The good news is that there is now plenty of malt whisky readily available and it is a very rare pub or off-licence where you cannot get a Glenfiddich or a Glenmorangie (an exceptionally fine malt in my opinion). Many have up to a dozen or more. When I am in Liverpool I buy my own on draught from a little off-licence on the Aigburth Road – beautiful old Macallan at six pounds a pint. And no, I won't give you the address. But if you live in, or visit London, you can buy any malt that's currently bottled – and some that aren't – at Milroy's in Greek Street. You might even be advised by Wallace Milroy, who has forgotten more about malt whisky than I ever knew.

Malt whisky is not cheap – except if you

live in Liverpool or, I'm told, Sheffield, where it can also be bought on draught. The cheapest bottle normally costs about £10, although you can buy excellent malt whiskies at Tesco's, Sainsbury's and other chains at less than this. Though I must tell you that these malts are frauds – big name malts masquerading under other labels. At the top end of the market, the sky's the limit. You can buy a 46-year-old Linkwood for £36, and the last time I heard of it the 1938 Macallan was selling at £600 a bottle in Japan.

The bad news is that malt distilleries are being closed down at a frightening rate. More than twenty have gone in the last two years and three more went into mothballs a few weeks ago, including Glen Mohr at Inverness, of which the great malt whisky connoisseur Professor R. J. S. McDowall wrote, 'There certainly will never be a glut of delicious Glen Mohr.'

Prophetic words.

Sadly, while it is true that more malt whisky is washing about than ever before, the demand is just not making sufficient inroads into the large amount that was being distilled ten, fifteen and twenty years ago. One of the difficulties of the whisky trade is that you have to hold stocks and plan ahead for anything up to twenty years. Unfortunately, although malt sales are going up, total whisky sales are going down, and this market is so very much larger that it is really all that financially matters. And as I see from observing my own adult children, their tastes are for fruit salads with coloured umbrellas sticking out and called things like 'A slow comfortable screw up against a wall'. Young men no longer have to prove themselves by ordering Capstan Full Strength and a whisky and soda. Unless this situation changes – and I see no signs of it – I predict more distilleries closing their doors.

Happily, malt distilleries are not complicated buildings and a few months' – or a few years' – closure does not ruin them. Even the biggest malt distillery, Tomatin (and that's one of the ones that has recently closed) employs only a few dozen men and it takes only a skeleton staff to keep the stills, mash tuns and washbacks in good order. So closed distilleries can become working distilleries without much trouble. This happened a few years ago when one of Scotland's prettiest distilleries, Ledaig, opened up again and it is now producing a very decent malt renamed Tobermory – a much better name anyway.

And, to be fair, this is not the first time that malt whisky has seen hard times. A visit to Campbeltown on the Mull of Kintyre will tell you a sorry story. Not long ago, Campbeltown was the whisky capital of Scotland, with 32 distilleries within a stone's throw of each other. It could have been rightly called the whisky capital of the world. It is now a whisky graveyard, with only two distilleries left – Springbank and Glen Scotia, both, incidentally, producing excellent malts.

The story of Campbeltown is a sad one, a story of greed, opportunism, huge profits – and disaster. Because Campbeltown was – and is – ideal for making malt whisky. It has plenty of pure, cold water. It has peat. It had barley, skilled manpower and a tradition going back to the very beginning of malt whisky. Understandably, Campbeltown whiskies were famous for their quality and in the 1920s it seemed as though they could not produce enough to meet the demand. So the distilleries began to cut corners to produce more malt. The quality inevitably declined. The process was further accelerated by the introduction of Prohibition in America when all of a sudden Campbeltown could sell everything it produced immediately – no quality control, no proper casking, no maturing. There was no point in tying up valuable stock and capital if people didn't care what they drank. Fortunes were quickly made. Then, in short order, came the Great Crash of 1929, the Depression and – disastrously – the repeal of Prohibition. Once more there was a buyer's market and no one in America wanted the firewater that was all that Campbeltown was capable of producing. Even worse, the blenders in Scotland, who had the pick of the finest malts, were not interested. To build up decent stock again would have taken ten years, at the very least, and long before that the Campbeltown distilleries crashed.

Before you rush out to stock up in the face of all this gloom and doom I can reassure you that there is still plenty of malt whisky about – and plenty being produced. Certainly enough to see out anybody alive today. And it is becoming more and more popular as a fashionable drink all over the world. Long-term, this must be good news both for distilleries and drinkers.

Why is malt whisky superior? It is, generally speaking, older and so better matured. But, apart from this, it is demonstrably smoother, rounder, more characterful, with a cleaner, better nose and a more agreeable aftertaste. I take mine with a little water these days but it can be drunk neat with pleasure. Is Scotch malt the only malt produced in the world? By no means – although I believe it is the best. Avoid Australian and New Zealand. Avoid African and South American variants (they make no malt whisky in North America anyway). Avoid malts from behind the Iron Curtain. Avoid Italian malts. This is all homework I've done for you. Especially avoid malts from bottles shaped like eagles. But I'd put a good word in for the Japanese. Standard Suntory is, in my view, a perfectly palatable whisky. Along with Irish and the North American bourbons and ryes, it is – outside Scotch – one of the only decent whiskies you can drink.

July 1985

Alan Coren

THE HANGOVER IN QUESTION

4.17 am, light from fridge snaps on, reverberates through head like noise, can *hear* pupils contracting, shut fridge door, little polychrome rhomboids continue to kaleidoscope about in brain.

Or I am dead. This is Elysian fridge, I have snuffed it and gone to Kitchen, God's final jest, doomed to an eternity standing on jammy lino in bare feet, unable to find bottle opener, parched for Coke.

Would He be this tough on drinkers? Cannot recall pentateuchal injunctions against alcohol, is there an XIth Commandment somewhere in small print, *Thou shalt not booze?* Are there parables in minor prophet texts, *And Jeroboam came home legless, and fell over the cat, and uttered oaths; and the LORD God brought forth thunderbolts and smote him in that place where he was, saying: Henceforth shall the floor of thy mouth be as a wadi, and thine eyeballs as twin coals, and the fruit of thy loins go about on all fours, even unto the tenth generation?*

Amazing what a few minutes of natural sleep can do for you. Such as maim. Came home at 3.15, not tight, loosened, if anything, one or two joints unbolted, no more than that, perfectly capable of sticking key in letter-box and walking into Christmas tree, got glass ball off ear at only third attempt, negotiated staircase easily as falling over a log, found bedroom door handle well before 3.30, removed clothes with nothing more than minor pause to work out best way of pulling trousers over head, climbed athletically into bed, stubbed fag out on clock, sank into oblivion.

Rose from oblivion, 4.13, not tea-time already, surely? No, clock still smoulderng, faint smell of plastic molecules reorganising their domestic arrangements.

Tongue lying on mouth-floor like felled cactus.

Got up, carrying head carefully in both hands, groped for dressing-gown, dressing-gown totally incapacitated, arms flapping, belt treble-knotted, dressing-gown obviously just got in from even wilder New Year's Eve party than mine, crawled downstairs together like, like, like – who was it used to sing *Me and My Shadow*, plump man, white tie, face of some kind?

4.20, now, by kitchen clock; brave fridge searchlights again, Guy Gibson's voice crackling on ectoplasmic intercom as we go in low over the bacon, something registers a hit on hand, grab Coke bottle from back of fridge, slam door, and we are away before gunners can even get range.

What hit hand? Hand got egg-white on it. Two possibilities: either I bleed albumen, or else wife still pursuing mad habit, despite previous incidents, of leaving egg-white in cup after using yolks, standing cup on top shelf, and awaiting results.

Cannot bring self to open fridge again, know what it looks like, seen it before, it looks like giant snail has run amok; not generally known fact that average hen's egg contains up to eighteen miles of mucus if allowed to drip long enough.

Put it behind me, other things on what's left of mind, how, for example, to open Coke bottle? By light chiaroscuring in from street lamp, as in Carvaggio's immortal *Parched Drunk Looking For Coke Bottle Opener*, begin tugging at utensil drawers, forgetting Second Law of Ergodynamics which states that all drawers stick during small hours, also forgetting Third Law of Ergodynamics which states that all drawers *only stick for a bit*.

Said bit having elapsed, all drawers leap from their cavities and vomit cake-cutters, used batteries, bent screwdrivers, half a scissor, corks, spare fuses, knife handles, flea collars, pieces of gas bill, empty Sparklets, flints, two-pin bakelite plugs you brought from your last house just in case, Good Boy drops, cup handles, matchboxes (empty), matchboxes (with screws in; or, after drawer flies open, with screws out), doll's heads and seventy-one keys you brought from yur last house just in case.

No bottle-openers, though.

4.26.

Think.

Have seen John Wayne open bottles with teeth. Or, no doubt. John Wayne's double's teeth. Probably special teeth, though, enamelled steel props built at San Diego Navy Yard. *John Wayne's double lies a-mouldering in the grave, but his teeth go marching on* . . .

Shall not chance own vulnerable choppers, though, last time I chomped an incautious cobnut, mouth resembled tiny Temple of Dagon, crumbling masonry everywhere, crown dust rising, bits of bridge, World War Two fillings – God knows what Coke bottle would do, whole skull might come off.

Ah.

Remember seeing somone open Coke bottle in door-jamb.

Ah.

Look at foot.

Foot still hissing slightly, Coke bubbles dying among instep hair. Must be special trick in opening horizontal Coke bottle in door jamb. Must be *two* special tricks, since large sliver of door jamb now lying beside Coked foot.

4.31.

No more Coke in house.

Water, squash, milk, no use, need something aerated, no good simply de-parching tongue, am Very Aware of need to shift something lying sideways across oesophagus. Seem to have swallowed large plank. Could be case for Red Adair, long experience assures me only megacharge of bubbles will do trick, no point ringing Dyno-Rod at 4.33, *You must be joking, squire, couldn't touch anything till February earliest, we're up to here with paperwork, not to mention staff shortages, unofficial strike up Northampton, black ice, Good Friday looming, etc* . . .

If plank *is* lying across oesophagus.

Aorta? Vasa cava inferior? Duodenum? Ventriculus dexter? Pulmo?

Stop, in larder, hand on bicarb packet; reflect.

All down to Jonathan Miller, this. We live in post-Body in Question Age. Used to know nothing about what goes on past tonsils. Now know three per cent. Point-three per cent. Know it looks like Rotorua mudspring, in constant state of peristaltic glug; know about referred pain, i.e. if feel sudden stabbing pain in shin, could mean going deaf. To layman – to 0.3% expert – entire nervous system is result of giant connective cockup, nothing hurts where it's supposed to, everything where it isn't. If Dalston Junc-

'He's the patron saint of drunks!'

complex or permanent germ-warfare battle-field. A great itinerant skin bag of blood and offal, horribly vulnerable. Never used to worry about smoking, drinking, guzzling, little men would take care of all that, scouring lungs, washing down intestinal tract, buffing liver to spotless health.

4.38.

Bicarb packet still in hand, plank still across throbbing insides. Eyes (not Box Brownies) focus on minuscule print: $NaHCO_3$.

Yes. Could be anything, really, could well combine with whatever I am to produce $SO_9C_4Pb_8Th_2Nb_6H_3Sb_2Zn_7$ ... not without unease, post-Jonathan, bunging assorted valences down into the pulsing tripes, what if wedged-plank-plus-aching-eye-plus-metal-tongue syndrome is actually referral of neurological complaints about dislocated spleen, could be $NaHCO_3$ is worst possible treatment for dislocated spleen, could end up quitting vale of tears on one terminal burp.

Appalling way to go.

Return bicarb to shelf, shut larder door, hobble across floor on Coke-gummy foot, fuses, screws, Good Boy drops sticking to sole, wedge plank grinding in chest cavity, possibly indicating grit behind patella, mastoid sprouting in left ear, onset of sili-cosis.

4.56.

Shameful, tragic, terrifying how body gets abused, body only thing I have (gave up idea of soul 1967, following TV programme by glib atheist), New Year less than five hours old, good time to make New Year Resolution, must stop punishing tissues, must give up fags, liquor, toast, fatty ...

Hang on.

Wonder if hair of dog good for wedged oesophagal plank?

Where scotch?

tion like that, Central Line tube to Chancery Lane ends up in East Kilbride.

Prior to Miller, all my anatomical information came from Arthur Mee. *Children's Encyclopaedia* used to have big sepia illustrations of human body in section, showing little men in overalls shovelling food into tin boiler (stomach), little men in head with Box Brownies (eyes), little men in lungs with foot-pumps. Very nice. Liked to think of them all down there, contented work force beavering away; felt like benevolent mill-owner, loyal workers whistling as they shovelled, pumped, treadled, ticked carbo-hydrates off clipboard check-list, stoked furnaces.

Pleasant, having anthropomorphic view of my own insides; every time I ate breakfast, thought of little men in spotless gumboots carrying egg away in buckets.

Impossible, now. Post-Miller, see myself as not even human, merely large biochemical

January 1979

'Nonsense, John – you give me the keys, I'll drive.'

'Turn the video up, John – I can hear myself think.'

Michael Heath

PUB CRAWLERS

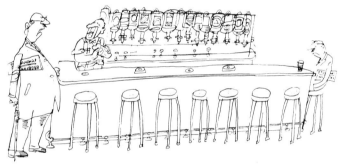

'Evening, Jim – who's the bastard sitting on my stool?'

'I like you, Bill – you're a bullshitter. So am I.'

'I can't remember which beer it was I saw advertised on television. There were these three yobs knocking pints of it back and looking very happy.'

THE BRITISH CHARACTER
A TENDENCY TO LEAVE THE WASHING-UP TILL LATER